DATE DUE

Cultural Autonomy in Global Communications

This solidly documented contribution to the search for new politics outlines a systematic, concrete program of communication development in Third World Nations. In a debate too often characterized by confusion and misunderstanding, this book clarifies the central issue: the attempt of Third World nations to maintain and develop their cultural identities. *Cultural Autonomy in Global Communications* analyzes some of the key problems in international communications:

- The importance of cultural autonomy for Third World development.
- The role of international communication in national cultural development.
- The erroneous and misleading conceptions of an emerging global information order.
- Formulating policies of self-reliance and alternative development in communications.
- Essential elements to be considered in national communication planning.

This book brings together some of the most advanced thinking on international communication policy important for students, researchers, and policymakers.

> "Hamelink analyzes important problems in the relationship of culture, information, and the economic order. This book is a valuable contribution to the international debate."
>
> Emile McAnany
> University of Texas at Austin

> "Most publications have pushed the pendulum of thinking on global communications to one extreme or the other. Seminal thinkers like Cees Hamelink have tried to bring about some balance in the debate. This book is a most opportune and welcome effort."
>
> K.E. Eapen
> University of Kerala, India

> "Cees Hamelink's volume is a provocative, unorthodox, and insightful work in the area of cultural autonomy and communication."
>
> Hamid Mowlana
> The American University

COMMUNICATION

AND HUMAN VALUES

A series developed by the Centre for the Study of Communication and Culture, London, England, in cooperation with the World Association of Christian Communication, London.

Cultural Autonomy
in
Global Communications

Planning National Information Policy

Cees J. Hamelink
Institute of Social Studies
The Hague

Longman
New York & London

CULTURAL AUTONOMY IN GLOBAL COMMUNICATIONS
Planning National Information Policy

Longman Inc., 1560 Broadway, New York, N.Y. 10036
Associated companies, branches, and representatives
throughout the world.

Developmental Editor: Gordon T. R. Anderson
Editorial and Design Supervisor: Ferne Y. Kawahara
Manufacturing Supervisor: Marion Hess

Library of Congress Cataloging in Publication Data
Hamelink, C. J.
  Cultural autonomy in global communications.

  (Communication and human values)
  Bibliography: p.
  Includes index.
    1. Communication policy.   2. Communication, Inter-
national.   3. Underdeveloped areas — Communication.
I. Title.   II. Series.
P95.8.H35   001.51   82-15299
ISBN 0-582-28358-2   AACR2

Manufactured in the United States of America

The Truth is, however, that the oppressed are not marginals, are not men living "outside" society. They have always been inside — inside the structure which made them "beings for others." The solution is not to "integrate" them into the structure of oppression, but to transform that structure so that they can become "beings for themselves."

Paolo Freire
Pedagogy of the Oppressed

Contents

Foreword

The strength as well as the most salient feature of capitalism, as Wallerstein has shown, is that it is an international system. The maintenance
of a world sector is essential to its well-being and survival. That sector is
comprised of nation states with great economic disparities between and
within them.

In recent years, world capitalism has become increasingly reliant on
communication technology and information flows to maintain and defend its position. Transnational corporations, the chief organizers of the
world business system, have become vitally dependent on information
flows to carry on their operations and to sell their goods and services in
the international market. An influential U.S. publisher is emphatic
about this:

The stakes in the coming battle (over a new international information order) go
far beyond editors and publishers, who, so far, have been the only ones directly
involved. They extend to the great computer and information hardware companies whose foreign sales of billions of dollars are at stake; to the TV networks
and movie makers whose entertainment products range the globe; to the
airlines and banks and financial institutions whose need for computer-to-
computer data literally defines their business; to the multi-million dollar advertising industry.[1]

Then there is the military's dependence on the most sophisticated
and advanced communication systems to enable it to perform its assigned task of ensuring the continued security and operation of the

worldwide business system. And, finally, there is capitalism's global ideological front to be taken care of, also dependent on communication technologies and information flows. A recent U.S. State Department assistant secretary put it this way: "Unless we, in government, are sustained by a coherent and aggressive national communications effort, we could find ourselves becoming irrelevant and ultimately overmatched in the ideological battles ahead."[2]

A governmental report is no less blunt: "If the United States is not to lose its leadership in world information industries, the U.S. Government must commit greater resources to the problems of international telecommunications and information flow."[3]

The world business system, with U.S. corporations as managers and "leaders," seeks to tie as much of the world as possible into the transnational economic order. Capital export, banking and financial connections, and advanced communication technologies are some of the most prominent and important means by which the world business system expands and broadens its control.

The prescriptions found in Cees Hamelink's book collide frontally with the vital interests of the transnational corporate system. In his plea for "cultural dissociation," Hamelink urges that nations seeking sovereignty and independent development sever as many as possible of their links, especially cultural and informational ones, with the transnational corporate chain.

Fine advice! But Hamelink is well aware that the modern world system is tied together by more than movies, TV shows, and news flows. There are dense economic networks utilizing transoceanic cables, satellites, interpersonal connections, and interactive computers that facilitate an historically unprecedented international corporate economic order. Accordingly, there is no chance that a new international information order can be gained independently of and separately from the transnational economic system now dominating. The players in this engagement are not journalists and poets. They are Exxon, IBM, and General Motors. And they are playing for multibillion-dollar stakes.

Thus, whereas Hamelink calls for dissociation, the transnational response is to create "interdependencies" as rapidly as possible — in production, finance, and communications. At the same time, the North American center, concerned with rising resistance to all forms of domination — economic, cultural and military — in peripheral areas makes no secret of its intent to *fight* to prevent further erosion in the empire.

The announcement by the newly elected president of the United States in early 1981 of an armament expenditure program of more than a trillion dollars ($1000 billion) for the 1981–1985 period is only a more recent example of reliance on a military response to the problem. His secretary of defense, claiming the standard justification of empire-related atrocities on the basis of external threat, states: "We cannot deter that effort from seven thousand miles away. We have to be there. We have to be there in a credible way."[4]

At the same time, it must be admitted that to date the trans-nationals have been quite successful in promoting their integrationist program, one that they enjoy calling "interdependence." Simultaneously, their armed forces are everywhere gearing up to intervene should the "dissociation option" be taken up.

One fact is clear. The world business system has not contained the movements toward national independence that have grown up during the past four decades. Battles will become more intense. The most recent struggles in Nicaragua and El Salvador are not exceptional developments.

Yet it must be also acknowledged that when the armed struggles for dissociation succeed—and it seems difficult to imagine success without such struggle—enormous problems remain in the way of maintaining dissociation as a long-term course.

Wallerstein points this out:

Everywhere, the reality has been that the fact that a movement proclaims the unlinking of a state's productive processes from the integrated world-economy has never in fact accomplished the unlinking. It may have accomplished temporary withdrawal which, by strengthening internal production and political structures, enabled the state to improve its relative position in the world economy.[5]

Though this has been the historical experience, Wallerstein does not find it a cause for discouragement. He also observes that there is "the spread effect." The movements that have attempted to change the relation and conditions of their dependency have inspired others. "Mobilization has bred mobilization." And, no less important, the success of one movement—limited as it may be or even eventually reabsorbed—creates more opportunity for the next surge against the system. Though the world business system possesses enormous recuperative and absorptive power, each thrust against it creates more space and energy for later thrusts. Can it be disputed that this is a time of intensifying continuous pressure against domination?

Seen in this perspective, there is much merit in Hamelink's call for dissociation. However partial, and perhaps even fated to fail, any struggle for dissociation from the world business system is yet another pressure point against the still-prevailing international order of domination.

It should also be recognized that dissociation is a relative concept. It cannot be evaluated with some narrow cost-benefit calculus. It takes its honorable place in the long historical movement toward what Wallerstein sees as "the slow construction of a relatively free and relatively egalitarian world." Cees Hamelink's work is a contribution in this same process.

Herbert I. Schiller

La Jolla, California

REFERENCES

1. Philip H. Power, "Threat to Ad Freedom?" *Advertising Age*, 15 December 1980.
2. Sarah Goddard Power, "The Communications Revolution," U.S. Department of State, Bureau of Public Affairs, Current Policy 254, 5 December 1980.
3. *32nd Report: International Information Flow, Forging a New Framework*, 96th Congress, 2nd Session, House Committee on Government Operations, House Report No. 96-1535, 11 December 1980, p. 36.
4. Richard Halloran, "Weinberger Urging Sharp Outlay Rises in Military Budget," *The New York Times*, 5 March 1981, p. 1.
5. Immanuel Wallerstein, "The Future of the World-Economy," in Terence K. Hopkins and Immanuel Wallerstein (eds.), *Processes of the World System*, Beverly Hills, Sage, 1980, p. 176 and passim.

Preface

Human life is characterized by a great variety of cultures. They are not only the fascinating adornment of human history but also the crucial condition of human survival. Cultural diversity reflects the varying ways in which human beings adapt to their own specific and often unique environments.

In recent years, however, this delicate process of adaptation is being increasingly threatened by the large-scale export of the cultural system of the advanced industrial states to the countries of the Third World. As a result, the survival of autonomous cultural systems in many areas of the Third World is very much in question. It is the argument of this study that cultural autonomy is essential for a process of independent development. However, cultural autonomy is virtually impossible in a system which attempts to integrate the weak and poor countries in a global community that serves best the interests of only the rich and powerful. This autonomy has to be secured through the formulation and implementation of national policies based on international *dissociation* which encourage self-reliant development and the cooperation of developing countries among themselves.

The recent debate on proposals for a new global economic and information order is causing a fundamental rethinking of our ideas on development. The evident inadequacy of the current dominant models of development, especially in the area of information, calls for fresh, exploratory approaches. It is not the primary intention in this study to present a comprehensive survey of current literature on the issues of cultural dependency and autonomous development. Nor is this intended to be an introductory textbook in international communication. Rather, it is written as a documented contribution to the search for new policies which may ensure a more adequate participation of the Third World in the international exchange of information.

The current discussion on the new international information order has stirred strong controversy. Initiatives taken in this field by Third World countries have been described by Western media as "Orwellian mind control." But for Third World countries such efforts to shape a new international information order are an essential part of their total liberation. The present proposal for planning national information policies in a way that protects and stimulates the cultural autonomy of Third World countries will also undoubtedly be interpreted in some quarters as controversial.

When reference is made to the demands of Third World countries to restructure fundamentally the present international information exchange, I have chosen to use the term "new international information order." For reasons that are explained in Chapter 3 this term is preferred over such formulas as "new world information and communication order."

There are always more people that have inspired the author than can be listed in a preface. Some, however, have played an exceptionally large part and deserve to be singled out. In the preparation of the manuscript the criticisms and suggestions offered by Raquel Salinas, Herbert Schiller, and Robert White were very helpful and stimulating. I am also grateful for the meticulous work that Paul Kenney did on the references and the bibliography.

Cees J. Hamelink

1

Cultural Autonomy
Threatened

Every type of human society is characterized by the necessity to adapt to its environment. For this adaptation human beings develop a series of direct and indirect relations with their environment. The indirect relations constitute the cultural system of a society. This system comprises three types of adaptive relations:

- Instrumental: the instruments (techniques) human beings develop and apply
- Symbolic: the symbols with which human beings communicate
- Social: the patterns of social interaction which people create to carry out the varied tasks of life

The development of these adaptive relations is an inherent aspect of every society's struggle to survive. Crucial for survival will be the adequacy of a cultural system vis-à-vis the environment in which a society finds itself. Different climatic conditions, for example, demand different ways of adapting to them (i.e., different types of food, shelter, and clothing).

The adequacy of the cultural system can best be decided on by the members of the society who face directly the problems of survival and adaptation. They are in the best position to strike the balance between a society's environment and its material and immaterial resources. Critical for a society's chances of survival are the internal capacity and external freedom to develop its cultural system autonomously. Cultural

1

autonomy is fundamental to the independent and full development of every society.

Since environments in which societies have developed have always been diverse, we are confronted in human history with a great variety of cultural systems. Today, however, we see the rapid disappearance of the rich variety of techniques, symbols, and social patterns developed under conditions of relative autonomy.

A quick review of my own experiences of the international scene amply illustrates this point.

- In a Mexican village the traditional ritual dance precedes a soccer match, but the performance features a gigantic Coca-Cola bottle.
- In Singapore, a band dressed in traditional Malay costume offers a heart-breaking imitation of Fats Domino.
- In Saudi Arabia, the television station performs only one local cultural function—the call for the Moslem prayer. Five times a day, North American cops and robbers yield to the traditional muezzin.
- The incredibly rich local musical tradition of many Third World countries is rapidly disappearing under the onslaught of dawn-to-dusk North American pop music.
- For starving children in the Brazilian city of Recife, to have a Barbie doll seems more important than having food.
- In Senegal, a mobile video unit intended to produce popular programs in the village stands idle; the producers of local programs prefer the expensive studio modeled after Western standards.
- In South Africa, skin cream is available that lightens a black complexion. Advertising suggests that black cannot be the ideal of beauty.
- For the poorest people of Latin America, advertising is an important source of information. North American agencies tell them that the good life is the life of the average consumer in the U.S. Venezuelan housewives are encouraged to identify their happiness with possessing a refrigerator or dishwasher. Advertisements advise the worker in Bogota to escape from the daily routine by means of a U.S.-made Ford or a U.S. airline.
- Nigeria announces a Western color television system when the cost of a black and white set would absorb the annual income of an average farmer.
- On the Indonesian isle of Bali, performers of traditional Ramayana ballet increasingly adapt their presentations to the taste and comprehension of Western tourists.

- U.S. television entertainment fills in large portions of air time in many countries. Moreover, local programs are produced according to U.S. formats. Even small television networks in poor countries unquestioningly follow the Western example of broadcasting as many hours as possible. Some try to fill 6 to 10 hours daily. Such a practice then pushes these networks into the open arms of Theo Kojak and Starsky and Hutch. Where the production of an authentic local program may cost $1000, the local station owner may import North American culture for less than $500.
- In Central America, school children read in their U.S.-produced textbooks that the Indians living in lands with large gold deposits did not realize its value until the Spaniards told them. In gratitude, the Spaniards taught them reading, writing, and belief in God. The Indians began to work for the Spaniards voluntarily.
- Many broadcasts from All India Radio are loyal copies of BBC models. The most important Indian newspapers could have been edited in England. The Indian film industry followed the Hollywood path by becoming caught up in the Western preference for sex and violence.
- In its gigantic advertising campaign, IBM assures Navajo Indians that their cultural identity can be effectively protected if they use IBM typewriters equipped with the Navajo alphabet.
- In Algeria, the influence of the French language continues to be so strong that the daily *El Moudjahid* sells ten times more copies of the French than the Algerian edition.
- The millions of copies of Latin American women's magazines disseminate the North American ideal of the efficient, well-dressed, nonpolitical housewife and homemanager.
- In many Third World countries, babies die because imported milk powder replaces efficient and cheap breast-feeding.

This summary is only a selection of the images that thoughtful people in the Third World are increasingly confronting. These observations reflect a trend of cultural awareness that has been well documented in a series of studies.[1] Admittedly, we need more research on precisely *how* the process of cultural "imports" affects the receivers in the long term, especially with respect to cultural norms and behavior.

One conclusion still seems unanimously shared: the impressive variety of the world's cultural systems is waning due to a process of "cultural synchronization" that is without historic precedent. It appears that public recognition of cultural diversity is kept alive only on the folkloric level when traditional ceremonies, flags, and dress adorn international gatherings.

Throughout history, cultures have always influenced one another. The richest cultural traditions emerged at the actual meeting point of markedly different cultural patterns, such as the Sudan, Athens, the Indus Valley, and Mexico. The result of such confrontations, as in the case of African and Arab traditions, was an enriched — not destroyed — culture.

With few exceptions, the cultural history of humankind is not characterized by one-way traffic in cultural confrontation. To be sure, there have been notable and decisive exceptions, as is clear from the destruction of the Aztec and Inca cultures or the Brahmin kingdom of Champa.

But the more general characteristic is that cultural systems either maintain their integrity or develop a more pluralistic and richer pattern. For example, in the process of a two-way exchange, dominant nations with more primitive cultural systems may adopt the more refined systems of the nations they conquer. One illustration is that of Germanic kings who tried to convey classical Roman culture to their people after seizing power in the western Roman empire.

Moreover, in the interaction between "high" and "low" cultures, the latter is often far from passive. In many instances, the bearers of the low culture will actively and selectively adopt only certain cultural traits from the other culture. Some Indian tribes incorporated the Spaniards' use of horses; others, like the sedentary Pueblo Indians, did not.

In many cases, even the great empires of history have allowed dominated peoples their own cultural systems. Often this was a conscious strategy for the maintenance of their position of power. Such a procedure is evident in European colonial history, where the distance between the exclusively Western culture and the indigenous culture is kept as wide as possible.

In the second half of the twentieth century, a destructive process that differs significantly from the historical examples given above threatens the diversity of cultural systems. Never before has the synchronization with one particular cultural pattern been of such global dimensions and so comprehensive. Never before has the process of cultural influence proceeded so subtly, without any blood being shed and with the receiving culture thinking it had sought such cultural influence. It is remarkable that this process should happen exactly when technological development seems to facilitate optimal possibilities for mutual cultural exchange. Modern communications technology is offered to the world with the suggestion that the expression of cultural diversity is now definitely guaranteed. In reality, however, all the evidence indicates that centrally controlled technology has become the instrument through which diversity is being destroyed and replaced by a single global culture.

In international relations the preservation of cultural identity is increasingly a decisive issue. Cultural influence is now a central aspect of the military, political, and economic expansion of the Western industrial states; analysis of cultural penetration provides an essential key to understanding the mechanisms of the international metropolis-satellite structure. "The fundamental metropolis-satellite structure has remained the same throughout, but the basis of metropolitan monopoly has changed over the centuries."[2] This observation by André Frank accurately reflects the experience of many developing countries in the past half century. In the period of colonialism, the dependent satellites were kept under metropolitan control by political and military measures. After the formal recognition of their political independence, political-military coercion became the exception rather than the rule, with some notorious exceptions, such as Guatemala (1954), the Dominican Republic (1965), and Vietnam.

For many nations of Africa, Asia, and Latin America, the post-colonial period cannot be labeled independent, because of the effective maintenance of the dependency structure by such economic tools as loans, aid, investments, and trade conditions. In addition to this economic element, in the second half of this century there is a growing importance of yet another—and in the long run stronger—basis of the metropolis-satellite structure: the mechanism of cultural synchronization.

In the international literature, this phenomenon is usually described as cultural imperialism. I give preference to the concept of cultural synchronization, which is more precise for my purposes. In my view, cultural imperialism is the most frequent, but not exclusive, form in which cultural synchronization occurs. Cultural synchronization can take place without imperialistic relations constituting the prime causal factor or even without any overt imperialistic relations. The latter is illustrated by the adoption in the Soviet mass media of so many Western symbols and production formats.

Exogenous influence may be imposed on the receiving cultural systems or it may be actively invited by them. It is important to stress that even in the latter case, the synchronization with a foreign cultural system will very profoundly affect a society's long-term independent development.

The process of cultural synchronization implies that a particular type of cultural development in the metropolitan country is persuasively communicated to the receiving countries. Cultural synchronization implies that the traffic of cultural products goes massively in one direction and has basically a synchronic mode. The metropolis offers the model with which the receiving parties synchronize. The whole process of local social inventiveness and cultural creativity is thrown into confusion or is definitely destroyed. Unique dimensions in the spectrum of human values, which have evolved over centuries, rapidly disappear.

If cultural autonomy is defined as a society's capacity to decide on the allocation of its own resources for adequate adaptation to its environment, then cultural synchronization is a massive threat to that autonomy. Global cultural synchronization locates decisions regarding the allocation of resources extraterritorially. Exogenously developed techniques, symbols, and social patterns are introduced more on the basis of the interests and needs of the metropolis than on the needs and environment of the host country. The indiscriminate adoption of foreign technology can obviously produce profound cultural effects. For example, agricultural mechanization has influenced decisively the allocation of labor resources and, in turn, the pattern of life of large parts of the labor force.

Most striking — and central to the concern of this study — is the *scale* on which the cultural systems of Third World "satellite" countries have over the past three decades adopted techniques, symbols, and social patterns from the highly industrialized metropolitan countries. The transfer of culture from metropolis to satellite is historically not a new phenomenon; but since the 1950s, it takes place in an unprecedentedly large manner. The 1950s were the years of significant transnational expansion of capitalist economies and decisive transnationalization of industrial production.[3] The agents of the metropolitan economy, specifically the transnational corporations, are introducing throughout the world a revolution in commercial thinking: the world should be seen as one economic unit.[4]

The transnational firm no longer recognizes the validity of the autonomous national state or national culture. Consequently, as Jacques Maisonrouge, IBM president of the European division, states: the basic conflict of this new period is "between the search for global optimization of resources and the independence of nation-states."[5] Transnational firms consider national boundaries politically, economically, and culturally obsolete and unable to define business requirements or consumer trends. The world is one marketplace and the world customer is essential for that market. World market and world customer demand an optimal synchronization of cultural values so that authentic national characteristics do not jeopardize the unity of the transnational system.

The satellite countries therefore are incorporated in the transnational system by the persuasive marketing of cultural values that legitimize metropolitan interests. The concept of development, for example, is marketed in its equation with the concept of modernization.[6]

The developed nation is the modern nation that achieves the per capita income and the rate of mechanization and urbanization of the advanced industrial state.

In this move toward strengthening the cultural basis for the international dependency structure, the communication industrial complex is a vital element. The international flow of communications has, in fact, become the main carrier of transnational cultural synchronization.

Cultural synchronization and its function in the maintenance of the metropolis-satellite structure cannot be understood without knowledge of the role of the ruling class in the satellite countries. The class of internal colonialists is the crucial link between foreign interests and the exploited masses. A notorious example is the traditional elite of Latin American society — wealthy families who own the national newspaper chains and benefit greatly from alliance with the transnational corporations.

A classic example of the relation between a local elite controlling the media and transnational communication interests is the situation faced by Allende in Chile when he was elected in 1971. A major part of Chilean magazine publishing was dominated by the Edwards family, who also owned the influential and widely circulated newspaper *El Mercurio* and had exclusive rights for the AP, Reuters, and Agence France Presse news agencies. Edwards was president of the Inter American Press Association; the president of the Edwards group was at the same time president of IBEC (International Basic Economy Corporation). "Through this stock company, numerous national firms were controlled by North American investors, the majority of whom belonged to the Rockefeller group."[7]

The national elite provides the nationalist legitimization of the dependency system, the local marketing knowledge, and the "native" capital, which represents in many dependent countries an increasing share of industrial investment. Nationally dominant classes are the convenient intermediaries for the global spreading of a profit-oriented mercantilistic and consumer culture.

One must be aware that cultural influence through the communications industry does not always occur in a direct way. Many people in Third World countries are scarcely touched by the modern electronic and print media. Television, newspaper, films, and books are still inaccessible to millions of people in Africa, Asia, and Latin America. It is the urban elite and middle class who are most exposed to the North American influence on the local communication industry. If the ruling elite accept the imported social models, however, their action will certainly be decisive for the economic and cultural environment of the rest of the population.

Historically, industrialization has transcended the national borders and become global. In this transnationalization, the configuration of cultural values is inevitably mediated on a global scale, becoming the cultural basis in dependent countries for reproducing the modes of production, distribution, exchange, and consumption of the metropolis. As part of this global marketing system, the cultural commodities manufactured in the metropolis—films, television series, pop music—are massively exported to be reproduced, distributed, exchanged, and consumed in the satellite countries, thus competing with indigenous cultural values and cultural forms of expression.[8]

In the process of transnationalization, the public media are the major cultural institutions mediating the values inherent in industrialization. Their mode of mediation is generally synchronic. This means that in most social systems the public transmission of information and entertainment is guided by a concern to create a consensus regarding societal goals and their underlying values. This synchronization is made operative on a global scale by the transnational communications industry, which concomitantly with the transnational industrial expansion of past decades has extended the production and distribution of its goods and services from national to international markets.

Two factors are of vital importance in this process. On the one hand, in a number of branches of the communication industry, production for the home market remains the principal objective. Consider the examples of the international news agencies UPI and AP. Their most important market (between 60 percent and 70 percent of total revenues) is the public media in the United States; the production and distribution of their international product is thus guided primarily by the logic of the local national market.

On the other hand, some products of the communications industry, such as many of the television series, cannot hope to cover production costs with revenues from the home market alone. Costs for an average one-hour television drama, such as MCA's *McCloud, Baretta,* or *Kojak,* amount roughly to $400,000. Sales to television stations in the United States of America cover 75 percent of these costs, so that export becomes an evident necessity. Thus, a mass product has to be manufactured that has a sufficiently universal appearance to be salable anywhere in the world.

With the global expansion of the communication industry, television and film production companies, news agencies, advertising firms, and publishing houses have become transnational corporations of impressive scope. In their strategy of diversification, many industrial corporations have adopted communication as a profitable investment. Between 10 and 15 percent of the largest corporations in the world have considerable interests in the international communication trade.

Increasing concentration of economic power has developed, just as in other branches of industrial activity; 75 percent of today's international communication market is controlled by some 80 transnational corporations. These corporations introduce value patterns which are native to the metropolis but which have no relation to the genuine social needs of the receiving countries. One analyst notes that in Latin America, the foreign-dominated radio and television systems carry values that are alien to the real needs of those societies. Creation of social myths and false heroes and overemphasis on entertainment and violence are all instruments of alienation and cultural disorientation.[9]

Studies by the Finnish researchers Kaarle Nordenstreng and Tapio Varis indicate that entertainment is heavily represented in the one-way traffic of television programs in the world, which leads to a global spreading of cultural values that pervade the soap opera and crime series produced in the metropolitan nations.[10] The industrial corporations, however, provide more than just television programs; they also graciously entertain the world with films, records, cassettes, women's magazines, and children's comics. Illustrative examples of the last come from the Walt Disney Corporation. Although it is claimed that the characters in the comic strips are nonpolitical, a closer analysis shows that the fantasy world of Disney has a strong political orientation.[11]

Although the international communications flow tends to consist mainly of entertainment products, the role of international news in transferring values should not be underestimated. The selection of news by the few large international news agencies undoubtedly reflects the values of metropolitan countries. Most developing countries are dependent on this choice for their information on events outside their country. They receive international news as well as news about themselves via the news centers in New York, Paris, or London. "In the absence of a national news agency in Thailand, India receives only the American or British version of events in that country. How that keeps Thailand and India from understanding each other more deeply and readily is for those who know how to judge."[12]

The transnational communication-industrial complex is apparently characterized by an impressive variety of structures and contents; in fact, however, there is great uniformity. Both organizational structure and product are North American. Evidently the United Kingdom and France are also important exporters of media institutional patterns and products. The United Kingdom and France are subcenters of the North American communications industry, because their organizational structure and their media contents follow North American models (although there are French and British peculiarities that played an important role in the synchronization process occurring between these metropolitan subcenters and their own satellite countries). Moreover, in the Third

World there are media exporters of some scope, such as Egypt and Mexico, although their own programming content is basically an adaptation of North American examples. Even the socialist countries are following the North American lead in many respects, despite the relatively infrequent flow of communications between East and West.

Of the various reasons for North American domination, the most important is economic. The enormous size of the media market in the United States of America has made it possible to develop very large communications corporations. Ready access to finance capital, technology, and marketing channels have also been important factors in the rapid creation of operations on a large scale. Such a strong national base has facilitated the expansion into the international market. The active collaboration between the communications industry and North American political, financial, and military circles has further strengthened such international expansion. This combination of economic and political factors has made it possible for corporations based in the United States not only to exploit technological possibilities but also to determine the popular media formats. Thus, the communications industry in the United States was always one step ahead of the rest of the world, especially in the critical period after World War II. Other countries could be offered a ready-made model with prices so low that competition was excluded.[13]

In analyzing the process of cultural synchronization and the role of the communications industry in this process, one must take into account the wide range of content and format employed. These include not only news and entertainment but also educational materials, children's comics, women's magazines, recorded music, computer-based data systems, optical fibers, and satellite communication systems. For a clear illustration of how the process of cultural synchronization functions, it is helpful to analyze in greater detail two of its vital channels: transnational advertising and the transfer of communications technology.

TRANSNATIONAL ADVERTISING

> We are expanding our activities in the area of
> total communications.
>
> **J. Walter Thompson**[14]

The most striking example of a vehicle for cultural synchronization comes from the transnational advertising industry. In 1979, worldwide advertising revenues for the 50 largest agencies was $3.9 billion. Of these, the 10 largest agencies in the United States garnered some 46 percent of this amount in both domestic and foreign revenues (see Table 1).

TABLE 1 Top Ten Advertising Agencies in United States and World Income

TOP TEN AGENCIES IN U.S. INCOME
(U.S. Agencies: Gross Income in millions)

Rank	Agency	1979	1978
1	Young & Rubicam	$149.7	$118.1
2	J. Walter Thompson Co.	118.2	107.2
3	Ogilvy & Mather Int'l.	106.8	89.8
4	Ted Bates & Co.	93.4	54.9
5	Foote, Cone & Belding	95.9	75.7
6	Leo Burnett Co.	94.5	89.0
7	BBDO Int'l.	91.3	80.1
8	Grey Advertising	74.7	65.2
9	Doyle Dane Bernbach	72.1	64.5
10	McCann-Erickson	69.4	59.6

TOP TEN AGENCIES IN INCOME OUTSIDE U.S.
(U.S. Agencies: Gross Income in millions)

Rank	Agency	1979	1978
1	McCann-Erickson	$181.0	$151.1
2	J. Walter Thompson Co.	135.7	114.9
3	SSC&B	119.9	100.9
4	Ogilvy & Mather Int'l.	99.4	82.5
5	Young & Rubicam	97.9	85.8
6	Ted Bates & Co.	82.6	76.0
7	D'Arcy-MacManus & Masius	70.6	54.7
8	BBDO Int'l	53.5	52.3
9	Leo Burnett Co.	48.6	39.2
10	Campbell-Ewald	44.6	38.9

TOP TEN AGENCIES IN WORLD INCOME
(U.S. Agencies: Gross Income in millions)

Rank	Agency	1979	1978
1	J. Walter Thompson Co.	$253.9	$221.5
2	McCann-Erickson	250.4	211.0
3	Young & Rubicam	247.6	203.8
4	Ogilvy & Mather Int'l.	208.2	168.4
5	Ted Bates & Co.	181.0	133.1
6	SSC&B	153.2	133.1
7	BBDO Int'l.	144.8	120.4
8	Leo Burnett Co.	141.1	128.3
9	Foote, Cone & Belding	137.6	110.0
10	D'Arcy-MacManus & Masius	128.0	104.7

Source: *Advertising Age*, 19 March 1980, p. 1. Reprinted with permission of Crain Communications, Inc.

The top 10 North American agencies control 40 percent of their domestic market. Their leading international position is owing to the fact that the largest global advertisers are the best clients. The 10 largest clients are Procter & Gamble, General Foods, Bristol-Myers, American Home Products, General Motors, Unilever, Ford, Sears Roebuck, R. J. Reynolds Industries, and Colgate-Palmolive. These corporations spend on average 30 percent of their advertising budgets on the international market.

Transnational advertising is thus mainly propaganda for the products of the largest North American transnational corporations, propaganda designed and packaged by the largest North American advertising agencies. These major agencies are dominant not only in developed countries, such as Australia, where the top 10 U.S. agencies control 38 percent of the advertising market, or the Netherlands, where their control is 43 percent, but even more so in Third World countries, where over 70 percent of national advertising markets are controlled by agencies based in the United States.

The transnational advertising industry is characterized by *strong growth* — between 1970 and 1978, advertising budgets of the largest advertisers in the United States have doubled; *strong concentration* — of the 50 largest advertising agencies in the world in 1977, 36 have owners in the United States and account for 81.5 percent of the revenues of the 50; and *strong transnationalization* (see Table 2).

The most important channels for the advertising agencies in developing local markets are the public media. The international marketing strategy for the expansion of corporations based in the United States is therefore intimately linked with the export from the United States of the commercial radio and television model. An increasing number of countries have surrendered to the attraction of advertising revenues and allowed advertising to be part of regular radio and

TABLE 2   Participation of Foreign Advertising Agencies in National Advertising Sales (1975)

Countries	Percent Foreign	Joint Percent Venture	Percent National
Industrialized countries (minus United States)	42.1	7.1	50.8
Industrialized countries (including United States)	18.6	3.1	78.3
Third World countries	62.2	6.7	31.1

Source: "The Role of Trade Marks in Developing Countries," Geneva, UNCTAD, TD/B/C.6/AC.3/3/Rev.1, 1979, p.34.

television programming. In Third World countries particularly, advertising messages take up a considerable portion of broadcast time (see Table 3). In some Latin American countries, television advertising accounts for more than 25 percent of the total air time, principally because advertising films are a cheap way to fill expensive broadcasting time.

The messages produced and distributed by the transnational advertising agencies can be divided into two categories: informative and persuasive. Transnational industrial corporations will spend money mainly on advertising for *consumer goods* such as detergents, prepared foods, etc. Compared with total sales, a high percentage is spent on advertising. The largest United States producers of consumer goods spend an average 6 percent of their sales budget on advertising; considerably less money is spent on advertising for *capital goods* such as heavy machinery, office equipment, lorries, etc. The largest United States producers of capital goods spend an average 0.8 percent of their sales budget on advertising.[15]

It is important to observe that the advertising for consumer goods is generally of a persuasive nature. This means that for goods requiring the greatest amount of information, the actual informative content of the advertising about them is the smallest. For capital goods, however, where the target audience is usually rather well-informed, the informative content of the advertising is very significant. Take, for example, the detailed descriptions of machinery in advertising in trade magazines. Transnational advertising aimed at Third World countries, however, floods them with messages for consumer goods which inform very little but persuade very strongly.

The number of trademarks registered in Third World countries indicates the rate of their introduction and the source of foreign consumer goods. In 1974, 49.9 percent of the newly registered trademarks were foreign, compared with 27.4 percent in 1964.[16] These foreign trademarks come mainly from the highly industrialized countries (95 percent), especially the United States (34.4 percent), Japan (15.1 percent), United Kingdom (12.2 percent), and the Federal Republic of Germany (9.2 percent).

TABLE 3   Percentage of Airtime for Advertising

Countries	Radio	Television
Western	5.8	4.9
Socialist (Eastern Europe)	0.9	2.2
Third World	19.8	11.8

Source: "The Role of Trade Marks in Developing Countries," Geneva,
   UNCTAD, TD/B/C.6/AC.3/3/Rev.1, 1979, p.30.

More than three-quarters of these new registrations concern consumer goods: chemical products (16.2 percent), food (11.2 percent), tobacco (3.2 percent), textiles (12.8 percent), and, especially, pharmaceutical products (16.7 percent). In the case of this last category, it is striking that the same product is often sold under many different trademarks. The advertising budgets in the pharmaceutical industry are exceptionally high, almost 30 percent of their sales budgets. Supported by extensive advertising campaigns, products are sold that falsely claim to have a quality superior to products lacking trademarks. As a consequence of these campaigns, the primary target audience, the medical doctors, get very little objective, reliable information. Many doctors are inclined to prescribe these pharmaceutical products on the basis of the advertising; they thereby risk prescribing ineffective products.[17]

Western pharmaceutical products are often grossly overpriced. In Sri Lanka, for example, a certain antibiotic was sold for US $17 per 1000 capsules; the state pharmaceutical institute discovered after testing that the same product could be purchased in its original form for US $6 per 1000 capsules.[18]

Advertising for the products from the largest United States producers of consumer goods contributes to the definition of basic needs in Third World countries. Products are not adapted to suit local needs; local needs, through advertising, are adapted to the products. Thus, consumption patterns are being created that lead to a wasteful spending of what little is available. The poorest in Third World countries spend a considerable part of their income for products which make them even poorer.

In many Latin American countries, peasant women are receiving training as "promotores de salud," a type of paramedic similar to the Chinese "barefoot doctors." After their course of instruction, the Red Cross gives them a basketful of products from Bayer, Ciba-Geigy, Merck Sharp and Dohme. These products will then be sold in remote villages. Often, however, the villages have very effective traditional herbal medicines at their disposal. In Bolivia, for example, advertising for Alka Seltzer has increased sales, even though there are more effective and cheaper alternatives, such as mint tea. In many areas of Peru, the population is thoroughly convinced that anything bought in the pharmacy has to be better than natural products. Every self-respecting family has Aspro, which they use with less knowledge and more unpleasant side effects than they do the naturally occurring medicines. Aspro is also far more expensive.[19]

Another example of abuses in advertising concerns the sale of tobacco. Cigarette sales in Third World countries have doubled over the past 10 years. The large transnational tobacco firms have discovered a rapidly growing market in these countries and strongly encourage the smoking of cigarettes through their aggressive advertising campaigns. A particularly striking fact is that the largest tobacco firm in the world, British-American Tobacco, sells cigarettes in Third World countries containing more nicotine than similar ones in domestic markets.[20]

A cultural system which would be adequate for the poorest persons in that system would mean a set of instrumental, symbolic, and social relations that helps them to *survive* in meeting such fundamental needs as food, clothing, housing, medical treatment, and education. Such needs are not met if they are identified with the consumption of Kentucky Fried Chicken, Coca-Cola, Aspro, or Peter Stuyvesant cigarettes.

Survival has to be stressed, because the introduction of inadequate adaptive methods is indeed a matter of life or death. This is most dramatically demonstrated in the case of baby food in Third World countries. Major producers of food products, such as Nestle, Cow & Gate, American Home Products, and Bristol-Myers, have made great efforts to advertise bottle feeding as the ideal type of baby food. Radio programs in native dialects and "milk nurses" have assisted in the successful advertising campaigns, which have instilled an almost magical belief in the white milk powder of the white man.

Replacing breast-feeding by bottle feeding has had disastrous effects in many Third World countries.[21] An effective, adequate, and cheap method has been exchanged for an expensive, inadequate, and dangerous product. The expense for the milk powder taxes an already strained family budget, sometimes up to 35 percent. Many illiterate mothers, unable to prepare the milk powder correctly, have not only used it improperly but have also inadvertently transformed the baby food into a lethal product by using it in unhygenic conditions. The baby food drama painfully illustrates how serious the contribution of advertising to cultural synchronization can be.[22]

Richard Barnet and Ronald Muller have described the impact of transnational advertising on Third World countries:

The world managers argue that they are cultivating tastes and educating for progress. Marketing the pleasures of becoming a man of distinction who knows and drinks good whiskey, of exercising power on the highway at the wheel of a new Fury, or escaping to the South Seas via Pan Am offers the people of poor countries the prospect of the "good life" to which they can aspire.[23]

This marketing strategy attempts to take advantage of the dreams of the poor of being identified with the rich. Barnet and Muller point to this in quoting studies by advertising consultant Professor Evangelina Garcia at the Central University of Venezuela. " 'They think that there are rich and poor,' she explained, 'but that all have access to the same consumer goods they hear about on the transistor or see on the TV. It is a matter of luck whether they have the money to buy them and luck can change.' "[24]

Advertising also brings about an identification with the culture of the more affluent social classes of the developed world. " 'An important impact of imported advertising campaigns,' Professor Garcia points out, 'is that values in the U.S. are reproduced in Venezuela, in relation to sex, love, prestige, race, etc. . . . Advertising,' she concludes, 'creates a psychological dependence.' "[25]

The acceptance by Third World countries of the patterns of consumption present in highly developed countries can also contribute to serious disturbances in the national economy, because these patterns demand a much higher level of individual and national wealth. As a result of this bombardment by advertising, the elite sectors, with higher incomes, tend to be integrated increasingly into the international economy, while the poor, spending scarce resources on unneeded things, lag farther behind in essentials such as health and education. This creates a widening gap between rich and poor and contributes to an explosive social disintegration. The important point is that transnational advertising does much more than sell products and shape patterns of consumption; it informs, educates, changes attitudes, and builds images.[26] In doing all this, transnational advertising contributes significantly to the cultural synchronization of the world.

TRANSFER OF COMMUNICATION TECHNOLOGY

Another major carrier of transnational cultural synchronization is the current form of transfer of technology. The control of technology is an essential element in global economic, political, and cultural relations. This control is monopolized by the largest industrial corporations, which have access to the funds for research and development and which are the proprietors of the majority of patents and licenses for technology. In many of the Third World countries, 60 to 90 percent of all patents are owned by foreign corporations. In the area of communications, research and development for all the new technologies, such as satellites, optical fibers, microcomputers, and laser beams, are controlled by a small group of the largest transnational aerospace and electronics corporations. The more conventional techniques, such as printing, are manufactured in only a few industrialized countries and have to be imported by most Third World countries. In many of the Asian, African, and Latin American countries, radio and television stations have been built by British, French, or United States corporations, which manufacture communications equipment. These same firms also instruct personnel in the use of the equipment, thus creating and maintaining Western standards of professionalism and organizational structure.

Contrary to many expectations, the volume and structure of technology transfer from metropolitan to satellite countries in recent decades has not contributed to the independence of the latter, but instead has often increased the dependence. In the case of Algeria, for example, the desire to speed up the development process through more effective telecommunications has meant that the whole national communications-infrastructure was in effect handed over to ITT, GTE, Ericsson, and Nippon.

With the transfer of technology, the following questions must always be posed: Which social group receives the economic, political, and cultural benefits? In the case of communication technology, it is especially important to ask, "Who benefits economically; that is, who gets more income from the application of new communications techniques?" Moreover, who benefits culturally? Who is going to use the new technology? Who can exploit their prestige value? Which groups can communicate more effectively by adopting this technology? In most Third World countries, past experience indicates that these benefits will accrue principally to three groups: the transnational corporations which deliver the products; the transnational banks which finance the purchase of the products; and a "new class" of officials—managers and military personnel connected with the ruling government who will be among the few able to use the products.

One of the effects of the process of technology transfer, as it is presently occurring in many Third World countries, is to create among ruling elites an identification with the cultural system of the exporting country.

Such an identification with a foreign culture has a number of important consequences:

1. A technology implies an institutional structure to support the administration, continued maintenance, and marketing of that technology. When a technology is imported, it is inevitable that at least some of the supporting social structure will also be introduced. The importation of the communication media is a classic example of how the whole institutional complex and administrative organization were brought in along with the supposedly "value-free" technology.

   Many countries, in choosing to adopt United States radio and television technology, have also introduced the United States model of commercial media. This structure was originally designed to suit specific United States commercial interests. The professional staff, which must maintain the hardware and produce the programming, receives a Western-oriented training and usually embraces Western professional norms. Along with this technical training, they internalize a foreign professional ideology and learn to define their social status in accordance with this ideology.

2. The communication technology introduced, such as around-the-clock television, is often very inappropriate for less-developed, largely rural countries. Television, for example, is useful only for a small urban elite; it places a priority on social services for this small elite instead of on the masses of rural peasants, who should receive the higher priority in national development.

   As was noted above, technology introduced from a developed country is more often oriented toward a sophisticated level of consumption rather than toward a solution to the pressing basic social problems. This aggravates the gap between rich and poor and enhances national disintegration.

   Moreover, the direct importation of technology impedes any effort toward using local resources and stimulating creative talents in the development of a technology appropriate for the specific conditions of that country.

3. At present, the transfer usually involves the end product of technology and not the knowledge which permits independent research and development and which is at the heart of technological control. The basic scientific and engineering knowledge is a commodity jealously guarded by corporate interests and treated as a proprietary right. What is at stake is a cultural value: the rejection of scientific and technological knowledge as a public good.

   Worthy of attention is the present tendency in industrialized nations, especially in the United States, to make easy access to scientific information, stored in public libraries, the private property of a few large data-processing firms. Only these firms have the financial and technical means to process, store, and retrieve the rapidly expanding volume of information available in the world today. The institution of public exchange of basic scientific knowledge is being replaced as this knowledge is reduced to a marketable commodity.

4. Finally, in the case of some kinds of technology, such as space satellites, the cost of research and development is so great that only the wealthier nations can afford it. Many Third World countries have no access to this more sophisticated technology or, if they do, it is under conditions of economic and political dependence.

   Often argued is that technology, such as satellite communication, is becoming less expensive over the years, so that

Third World countries are able to participate in its use. This is deceptive, because the facility of access to satellite communication via leased technology is not the same as having control over the communications system. There have been cost reductions in certain aspects of satellite communication, as evidenced by the figures in Table 4.

At the same time, however, the costs of launch and space vehicles have increased considerably during the period, so that control remains in the hands of the wealthier nations. In 1976, the seven space vehicles for the INTELSAT V series of satellites cost US$235 million to build and another US$273 million to launch. Since the vehicles themselves are not at their ready disposal, many Third World nations have decided to build earth stations and to lease transponders. Most commonly, the reasons given for this practice are the need for national integration and the improvement of educational and health-care systems. At present, Third World nations leasing transponder capacity from INTELSAT include Algeria, Brazil, Malaysia, Sudan, and Uganda. In the very near future, Colombia, Zaire, and Chile will be added to the list. Regional systems are being planned among the Arab nations and in Latin America.

Indonesia has its own satellite system with the Palapa I and II, manufactured by Hughes Aircraft, and now leases to other nations. Yet as a representative of Hughes Aircraft admitted, the Palapa system can be switched off when so requested by Hughes or the U.S. Department of Defense.[27]

The issue of transfer of technology has become particularly central, since recent international development strategies tend to seize upon this as the key mechanism for solving inequalities in international communications. In such forums as UNESCO, there seems almost unanimity regarding the necessity to transfer the technological resources from highly developed countries to the Third World in an effort to assist their

TABLE 4   Cost Reductions in Satellite Communication

Item	1965 Costs	1975 Costs
Earth stations	Several million $	$5,000 (for the ATS-6)
Network charge for one hour of prime-time transmission	$22,350	$5,100
Investment cost per circuit year in orbit	$32,500	$1,100

Source: Cees J. Hamelink, "Imperialism in Satellite Technology," *WACC Journal,* vol. 26, no. 1, 1979, p. 14.

integration into the global communications system. One may well ask, however, who exactly will benefit from this? There is a good chance, as will be argued later, that expanded global communications technology will be primarily to the advantage of transnational industrial and financial systems. The offer of direct technology transfer is attractive to many Third World countries, but seldom does the cost-benefit analysis take into consideration the potential threat to their cultural autonomy.

If the foreign technology is adopted, however, it necessarily influences the allocation of the receiver's resources. For example, the adoption of labor-saving automation technology greatly affects the allocation of human resources in the host country and tends to maintain the existing dependency relations.

In general, the key characteristic of the present volume and structure of technology transfer is the strengthening of existing dependency. Highly illustrative is the case of microelectronic technology and its impact on the international division of labor.

According to the doctrine of comparative advantage, it has been projected that whereas the developed countries with their advanced scientific knowledge would specialize in areas of high technology such as nuclear energy, space, and data-processing technologies, the Third World countries, using their low-wage advantage, would specialize in labor-intensive industrial production. A 25 percent share for the Third World in global industrial production by the year 2000 has even been foreseen on this basis.

There are, however, a number of problems with this projection.

1. The low-wage advantage of Third World countries is increasingly undermined by the higher level of productivity in the industrialized countries through the application of microelectronics. Automation makes labor costs a less important factor vis-à-vis investments in advanced equipment and top-level management.

2. There are already indications that industries which might have been expected to move to the Third World are likely to remain in the developed countries. The electronics industry, heavily involved in off-shore operations, seems to be planning new generations of plants in the industrialized countries as a result of automation techniques.

3. At present the Third World still offers an attractive reservoir of unskilled and semiskilled labor for the transnational corporations involved in the development and application of microelectronics technology. The mass production of consumer electronic goods frequently involves a large volume of standardized parts that can be assembled by semiskilled labor. Since the tech-

nology develops rapidly, products soon become obsolete, and in order to move items into the market quickly, it is important to keep costs low. Low wages for assembly are thus a vital factor. In the production of microprocessors (the "chips"), for example, the stage of assembly demands very little training and can easily be carried out in off-shore plants in the Third World. In contrast, design, production, and testing of the integrated circuits demands skilled labor and sophisticated equipment, all of which is handled in the home countries.

4. Another reason for maintaining or establishing production facilities in Third World countries are the "free trading zones" (FTZs). Many electronics manufacturers use these for their production processes. Presently, there are some 80 FTZs in the Third World and 40 more are about to be established. Half are located in India, Indonesia, Thailand, Malaysia, the Philippines, South Korea, and Taiwan. They offer many advantages to the transnational corporations, such as tax holidays, government subsidies, no free trade unions, no customs expenses, no restrictions on imports and exports, no currency controls, and so forth.

5. Many countries where the FTZs are located are expected to become important markets for electronic products in the 1980s and beyond. Many corporations will want to have production facilities near to these new markets.

The presence of transnational manufacturers of microelectronic products is often of very dubious benefit to the host countries.

1. In the electronics industry, the investments per laborer are relatively low, which makes it easy for the manufacturer to move the whole production process quite suddenly.

2. Approximately 80 percent of the labor force in the FTZs consists of women under 30 years of age, often recruited from peasant households. They are particularly desirable because of their delicate fingers, their working tempo, their readiness to carry out monotonous jobs, and their low salaries (half of what men would earn). In most FTZs, women live in miserable conditions in crowded barracks. When their usefulness ends, they are easily dumped.

3. Electronics technology usually becomes obsolete within about 3 years, which means that in case local plants take over, their products come late on the market and cannot compete with the transnational corporations that have meanwhile advanced considerably.

4. Again, as we saw before, there is no transfer of vital technological knowledge. The core of the microelectronics know-how remains firmly under the control of the large transnational corporations, which increasingly strengthen their positions by mutually restrictive agreements on technical information. Third World countries are left with a fragmented production process reduced to extremely simple routines. In this most advanced and very influential technology, the wealthier industrialized countries are carving out the niche that will serve their interests best.

THE CENTRAL THREAT TO CULTURAL AUTONOMY: CULTURAL SYNCHRONIZATION

In the debate regarding the emergence of a new international information order, a wide array of issues has been discussed: the representation of Third World countries in news reports in the First World; the domination of radio and television programming in poorer countries by foreign imports; the domination of the public media by commercial interests to the detriment of the real cultural and developmental needs of the country; and so forth. However, from the viewpoint of many Third World countries, the central issue is increasingly the threat to their cultural autonomy. This chapter has analyzed in depth why the threat to cultural autonomy is so serious and what are the major operative mechanisms of this threat.

The cultural system of a society is here seen as the totality of instrumental, symbolic, and social adaptive relations which have evolved so that the society can create a truly human existence within the variety of the world's environments. The autonomy of people in their cultural development, that is, the ability of people to respond according to their own best intuitions, is crucial in establishing an adequate cultural system.

Few, if any, cultures have developed as completely isolated phenomena; part of adaptive cultural growth is selective borrowing and exchange. In recent decades, however, there has arisen a process best described as cultural synchronization which threatens, as never before, the delicate balance of adaptive cultural relations in many parts of the world. Cultural synchronization implies that the decisions regarding the cultural development in a given country are made in accordance with the interests and needs of a powerful central nation and imposed with subtle but devastating effectiveness without regard for the adaptive necessities of the dependent nation.

The principal agents of cultural synchronization today are the transnational corporations, largely based in the United States, which are developing a global investment and marketing strategy. The transnational corporations which are most directly involved with the cultural component of this global expansion are the international communications firms. This chapter has summarized some of the major conclusions of the extensive research on the cultural penetration by those transnationals involved in global communications. Transnational advertising, however, and the current strategies of technology transfer constitute the greatest threat to cultural autonomy and are the two axes around which much of the global expansion of transnationals is centered.

Many countries are becoming increasingly aware of these threats to their cultural autonomy. The following chapter will examine the attempts of these nations to counter the mechanisms of cultural synchronization.

REFERENCES

1. See studies mentioned in the Bibliography under Culture and Imperialism.
2. A. G. Frank, *Capitalism and Underdevelopment in Latin America*, rev. ed., Baltimore, Penguin, 1971, p. 177. A pertinent selection from the large body of literature on the issue of imperialism and dependence would include the following: Samir Amin, *Unequal Development*, New York, Monthly Review Press, 1976; M. B. Brown, *The Economics of Imperialism*, Baltimore, Penguin, 1974; F. E. Cardoso and E. Faletto, *Dependence and Development in Latin America*, Cambridge, Mass., Harvard University Press, 1979; D. Chirot, *Social Change in the Twentieth Century*, New York, Harcourt Brace Jovanovich, 1977; C. Elliott, *Patterns of Poverty in the Third World*, New York, Praeger, 1975; A. Emmanuel, *Unequal Exchange*, New York, Monthly Review Press, 1972; J. Galtung, "A Structural Theory of Imperialism," *Journal of Peace Research*, vol. 8, no. 2, 1971, pp. 81-117; T. Heyter, *Aid as Imperialism*, Baltimore, Penguin, 1971; E. de Kadt and G. Williams (eds.), *Sociology and Development*, London, Tavistock, 1976; V. G. Kiernan, *America: The New Imperialism*, London, Zed, 1978; D. Nabudere, *The Political Economy of Imperialism*, London, Zed, 1977; H. Radice (ed.), *International Firms and Modern Imperialism*, Baltimore, Penguin, 1975; Jose J. Villamil (ed.), *Transnational Capitalism and National Development*, Sussex, Harvester, 1979; I. Wallerstein, *The Capitalist World-Economy*, Cambridge, Cambridge University Press, 1979.
3. Robin Murray, "The Internationalization of Capital and the Nation State," in H. Radice (ed.), *International Firms and Modern Imperialism*, Baltimore, Penguin, 1975, p. 128.
4. Richard Barnet and Ronald Muller, *Global Reach*, New York, Simon and Schuster, 1974, p. 18.

5. In an address to the American Foreign Service Association, Washington, D.C., 29 May 1969.
6. In the Western ethnocentric definition of development, social research (e.g., the work done in the 1950s by Wilbur Schramm, David Lerner, and Everett Rogers) has functioned as a sophisticated carrier of cultural synchronization.
7. Armand Mattelart, "Mass Media and the Socialist Revolution: The Experience of Chile," in George Gerbner et al. (eds.), *Communication Technology and Social Policy*, New York, Wiley, 1973, pp. 425-440.
8. For a more elaborate analysis, see Cees J. Hamelink, *The Corporate Village: The Role of Transnational Corporations in International Communication*, Rome, IDOC International, 1977, chap. 4.
9. Marco Ordonez, *Los problemas estructurales de la comunicacion colectiva*, Quito, CIESPAL, 1974, p. 6.
10. *Televisiontraffic: a One-Way Street?*, Paris, UNESCO, 1974.
11. Ariel Dorfman and Armand Mattelart, *How to Read Donald Duck*, New York, International General, 1975.
12. A. Mitra, "Information Imbalance," paper presented at ILET Conference, Mexico, 1976.
13. Jeremy Tunstall, *The Media are American*, New York, Columbia University Press, 1977.
14. J. Walter Thompson Advertising Agency, *Annual Report 1973*, p. 3.
15. Percentages calculated from data in *Advertising Age*, vol. 29, no. 9, 1977, p. 1.
16. "The Impact of Trade Marks on the Development Process of Developing Countries," Geneva, UNCTAD, June 1977.
17. M. Silverman, *The Drugging of the Americas*, Berkeley, University of California Press, 1976.
18. M. Silverman and P. Lee, *Pills, Profits and Politics*, Berkeley, University of California Press, 1974, chap. 6.
19. Information from field work by Jose Hulshof, Peru. Private correspondence, 1978.
20. Michael Muller, *Tomorrow's Epidemic? Tobacco and the Third World*, London, War on Want, 1978.
21. "Undoubtedly, the multinational companies, the manufacturers of formulas of milk products for infant feeding, have been aggressive in their advertising and their promotion of these products, and undoubtedly this has led to a great spread in bottle feeding of babies. I can without doubt say that the bottle feeding of babies has led to a great deal of ill health and many deaths." M. Latham, Medical Research Centre, Nairobi, Kenya, in an interview for the BBC television program *Panorama*, London, 1 December 1975.
22. Jane Cottingham, *Bottle Babies*, Geneva, ISIS, 1976.
23. *Global Reach*, p. 173.
24. Ibid., p. 175.
25. Ibid., p. 176.

26. Karl P. Sauvant, "The Potential of Multinational Enterprises as Vehicles for the Transmission of Business Culture," in Karl P. Sauvant and Farid G. Lavipour (eds.), *Controlling Multinational Enterprises,* New York, Campus Verlag, 1976.
27. See Robert E. Jacobson, "Satellite Business Systems and the Concept of the Dispersed Enterprise; an End to National Sovereignty?" paper presented at an East-West Communication Institute Seminar, Honolulu, Hawaii, East-West Center, 1978, p. 30.

2

Resistance to Cultural Synchronization: National Initiatives

I do not want my house to be walled on all sides
and my windows to be stuffed. I want the culture of
all lands to be blown about my house as freely as
possible, but I refuse to be blown off my feet by any
one of them.

Mahatma Gandhi

In many dependent countries, the importation of an inadequate cultural system is actively stimulated by a small leading elite and is passively accepted by the majority. A change in this process has been evident in recent years, with an increasing awareness that the imported culture is usually accompanied by such a high degree of dependence that the recipients are completely "blown off their feet."

The awareness that transnational cultural synchronization is an instrument for securing metropolis-satellite relations was clearly brought to the fore in 1973 during a conference in Algiers of non-aligned countries:

It is an established fact that the activity of imperialism is not limited to economic and political domains, but that it encompasses social and cultural areas as well, imposing thereby a foreign ideological domination on the peoples of the developing world.[1]

In reaction to this foreign domination, some countries have attempted to retain and develop further their own, more adequate, cultural system. This occurred not only in the Third World, where there is often almost total domination, but also in a number of industrialized countries. In Canada and Australia, for example, there is an increasing concern with the massive cultural imports from the United States. In the European Community, there have been proposals in support of indigenous film industries. Some Western European countries have initiated developments which foreclose the possibility of arbitrarily supplying North American computer firms with all kinds of personal information concerning their citizens.

In Sweden, transnational firms are allowed to transport only information (concerning financial status, health, criminal record, etc.) pertinent to Swedish citizens across the border after receiving special permission to do so from the government.

The French government has shown considerable concern, because their macroeconomic planning has become completely dependent upon data and economic models which are stored in a computer in Cleveland, Ohio, United States. This concern has manifested itself in legislation which purports to control international computer traffic and simultaneously to protect the national computer industry.

Underlying such initiatives is the view that even in the most advanced form of international information exchange (the flow of information from computer to computer via satellites, called "compunication"[2]), the threat of cultural synchronization is real. International compunication is primarily monopolized by a few North American firms upon which many countries are dependent for their economic decision making. These large companies are, in fact, alone in possessing the technological means to collect, process, and store the ever-increasing stream of political and economic data emanating from government and industry. Accordingly, an important part of national decision making is extraterritorially and centrally influenced by private enterprises.

In these attempts to resist cultural synchronization, the focal point is the protection of a nation's cultural system against foreign imports. This is often discussed in terms of the preservation of the sovereignty of national cultural systems.

The concept of national cultural system or national culture is in many ways a misleading one. One could even argue that in the strict sense of the word nation, a national culture hardly exists in Third World countries, given their brief existence as nations. In many cases, Third World nations are made up of social groups which were artificially created by the colonizing powers and brought together within national borders. What is usually referred to has to do with local traditional folklore: the set of instruments, symbols, and social patterns that link a society to its past generations. What is called and defended as national culture may, in fact, no longer exist. What once was an authentic cultural system may have completely vanished and be irretrievable.

Another problem, especially prevalent in many Third World countries, is that no single national culture exists; instead, there may be many local or tribal cultures, between which there is considerable tension. Under such conditions, stimulating the authentic cultural systems could be disastrous. Moreover, it is questionable whether authentic traditional cultural patterns represent, in every case, an adequate environmental adaptation.

Complicating the issue even further is the fact that national cultural characteristics are not necessarily being swept away by transnational corporations; on the contrary, in some cases these corporations use the indigenous culture to promote the sale of the products.

It is also important to note that what is purported to be the national culture is not the culture shared by the masses of the population but is often the lifestyle of a small, urban, foreign-oriented elite. In some cases, this elite, linked with corporations based in North America, has expropriated the external trappings of a national popular tradition but has commercialized it and in other ways cut it off from the real historical roots of the national culture.

In Mexico, the agrarian, native-oriented revolution of 1911-1924 brought forth a popular *agrarista indigenista* (Indian) literature, which found expression in a popular genre of art, novels, music, drama, and cinema. This artistic and literary expression has perpetuated an important value tradition in Mexico. Following North American formats, the entertainment industry in Mexico has, however, taken over this tradition for commercial ends and so transformed it that it is devoid of any real social or historical meaning for the Mexican people.

In Brazil, moreover, there has been a concern to establish a national cultural policy. The Brazilian government correctly ascertained that Brazilian television "has become a privileged vehicle for cultural importation, a basic factor in the denaturalization of our creativity."[3] The cultural policy of the Brazilian government, however, is largely representative of the aspirations of a small ruling elite. This kind of national culture leaves little room for the variety of cultural identities of the Brazilian people. Brazilian cultural policy, in fact, presupposes a national homogeneity which does not exist.

A similar process occurred in South Korea. In April 1976, Chung Hee Park's authoritarian regime announced that the national culture would be revived, partly by means of a massive cleanup. According to Park, South Korea was not to be polluted by foreign influences. Indeed, there had been a heightened interest in discovering national cultural history in South Korea, evidenced in the recent uncovering of royal graves dating back to the Silla dynasty, as well as attempts to revive traditional handicrafts. As was expected, however, this cultural renaissance fell in line with the political and economic interests of the ruling elite, in which case, the cultural revival was hardly based on a genuine national interest.

One cannot assume that cultural homogeneity exists within a country or that cultural differences are identical with political boundaries. The concept of national culture often does not take into consideration profound dissimilarities between ethnic groups and social classes within a nation; or cutting across national political limits, potential similarities between comparable social classes in other countries. This suggests that in examining aspirations toward a national culture, one must ask who is attempting to define the culture and what interests are involved.

Chile after the coup d'etat of 1973 is an example of widespread popular cultural opposition against a ruling elite. From the outset, the junta led by Pinochet implemented a policy of cultural repression. The teaching staffs of schools and universities were replaced; schoolbooks were burned; radio stations were shut down; censorship of books, newspapers, and magazines was instituted; artists were arrested, tormented, or forced to join the ranks of the unemployed; and journalists were murdered. Phonograph records of folk music were seized, especially those with Chilean revolutionary protest music; murals were destroyed. Indian musical instruments, such as the quena (a wooden flute) and the charengo (a sort of guitar), were forbidden as means of political expression.

Cultural resistance began immediately after the coup d'etat. It took the form of anecdotes, satirical songs, slogans written in washrooms and on the streets, pamphlets, murals, and clandestine newspapers, such as *Unidad Antifascista, Pueblo Cristiano,* and *Liberacion.* Cultural resistance also inspired performances in the peñas, a form of cafe-chantant; some of these, such as the peña Dona Javiera, became centers of the counterculture. The Chilean Ariel Dorfman points out, "All of these activities have one thing in common: they testify to a people's will to retain its identity, defend its dignity, and increase its knowledge."[4]

With the support of the church and other groups, a series of cultural activities was set in motion which covertly criticized the existing situation. Music festivals, poetry readings, theater productions, and art workshops were organized. On 8 March 1978, the Union of Radio and TV Actors organized a large cultural manifestation in solidarity with the imprisoned and missing persons.

Cultural resistance even plays an important part in concentration camps. Political prisoners write poetry, act in plays, make music, and produce handicraft products. Dorfman states, "The culture has an activating and inspiring effect upon a people after an attempt to rob it of its spirit. Every cultural occurrence is a victory, a new step towards further organization."[5]

As an expression of cultural sovereignty, national culture can be defined on various levels, in terms of various interests, and by various social classes. Both external and internal neocolonial regimes can define national culture so that it becomes an appropriate instrument for achieving their political and economic objectives. Progressive governments can find a definition of national culture which allows them to escape the metropolis-satellite relation of dependency. Liberation movements can develop a cultural expression which enables them to retain at least a modicum of identity in the face of mass repression. Accordingly, the key question is: When and how can cultural sovereignty be defined in an authentic, adequate manner?

"To fight for national culture means, in the first place, to fight for liberation of the nation," writes Frantz Fanon in an analysis of the Algerian fight for freedom.[6] Authentic cultural sovereignty is defined in the struggle for national independence: "A national culture is the whole body of efforts made by a people in the sphere of thought to describe, justify and praise the action through which that people has created itself."[7]

In the Algerian struggle against French rule, one can indeed see signs of cultural independence. Traditional symbols central to Algerian culture, such as the wearing of a veil, were adapted as symbols of the resistance against economic and cultural repression. Already in the 1930s, the French government, in an effort to destroy Algerian culture, attempted to discourage wearing the veil. It was thought that if women could be convinced to abolish this cultural pattern, the men could also be made to accept a foreign pattern of life. In this period, the wearing of the veil became an act of resistance against cultural synchronization.

Then, from 1955 on, women started participating actively in the revolutionary struggle. At this point, in order to support the resistance movement, the women of their own accord decided to take off the veil. By conforming to French expectations, Algerian women were above suspicion and were allowed to pass the patrol posts with loads of grenades in their handbags. When the French discovered this practice, the veil again became important as a means for escaping notice and for concealing weapons under its protection. At the same time, devices introduced by the French, such as the radio, were adapted as a means of internal communication in the movement of independence from France.[8]

A similar phenomenon occurred in Chile during the rule of Allende. In the working class districts of Santiago, North American television series were viewed with close attention; the symbols, however, were interpreted in accord with the prevalent resistance to North American influences. The roles of good and evil were reversed, so that the white policeman became the bad guy and the black criminal the hero. In the same way, local comics were also created by Chileans using Chilean personalities but within the format of the foreign comic strips as a means of creating awareness of foreign intervention in Chilean national affairs.

Resistance against being "culturally blown off one's feet" has a variety of expressions, such as a return to traditional religious habits, an activation of handicraft skills, and a renewal of creative arts. The more modern video tapes, transistor radios, and documentary films come into play as well.

Striving for cultural autonomy does not mean "stuffing the windows." Rather, it expresses the desire to exchange freely with all cultural systems. As Gandhi said, however, "I refuse to be blown off my feet by any one of them." Acquisition of an independent identity is thus of primary importance. As Fanon writes, "The consciousness of self is not the closing of a door to communication. Philosophic thought teaches us, on the contrary, that it is its guarantee."[9]

Cultural self-assertion means that social groups are able to find the techniques, symbols, and social patterns necessary to allow them to adapt adequately to their environment. It is important to note that by these means, traditional and authentic elements can be combined selectively with new foreign elements. The Algerians were able to adapt very effectively to the demands of their struggle against the French through their selective use of both radio and the veil.

Recently in Iran, where tradition is a weapon in the struggle against cultural synchronization, the use of the veil has again become important as an expression of resistance. A journalist of Iran's daily, *Ajandegan,* remarked that she was absolutely against wearing the veil and in favor of equal rights for men and women. If the veil could be used in the fight against imperialism, however, she would wear it.

In Mozambique, independent since June 1975, an important element of foreign culture has been used very effectively: the Portuguese language. Paradoxically, Portuguese has been both the instrument for the Mozambiquans' loss of identity and simultaneously the language of the liberation movement. The *Voice of Frelimo,* broadcasting from Zambia and Tanzania during colonial rule, brought news of the freedom fight in Portuguese. According to President Samora Machel, language should not be seen as a static element; based on the revolutionary use made of Portuguese by Mozambiquan revolutionaries, a language with a Mozambiquan personality should emerge.

It is misleading to describe resistance to cultural synchronization as simply an attempt to preserve a national culture. Given the aggressive marketing and control of global communications that the metropolis has, it is necessary to seek a content and expression which form a truly *adequate* cultural system. Such an autonomously developed cultural system can give people confidence in their strength and be a source of motivation toward independent social development.

In the analysis of resistance to cultural synchronization, the relation between a cultural system and its political economy poses a special problem, because historical models are often misleading. This is evident from European cultural history, in which autonomous cultural development almost always has concurred with a strong, independent political economy.

The most important cultural developments of the fifteenth century occurred at the courts of the Burgundian dukes, notably at the court of Philip the Good. Given his strong political and economic position, he was able to make his Flemish court an international cultural center. Artists from that court, such as Van Eyck, Van der Weyden, Binchois, and Dufay set the trends which all of Europe followed.

Also the Golden Age of The Netherlands is characterized by the combination of great prosperity and impressive achievements in such diverse areas as architecture, painting, science, and letters. The seventeenth-century Dutch painters and architects had an influence which extended far beyond their national borders.

In the seventeenth century, France, too, had significant economic growth, in part as a result of competition with The Netherlands. Jean-Baptiste Colbert inspired the government to extensive economic protectionism, which led to a blossoming of French trade and industry. This period was also that of the Sun King Louis XIV and his imposing baroque creation, the palace at Versailles.

England reached an economic high point in the nineteenth century. The Victorian style was developed during this period, manifesting itself in terms of a specific style of interior design, painting, and refined engraving methods. The Victorian era also marks the peak of British imperialism; England was the most powerful country in the world during the reign of Queen Victoria.

From this brief historical survey one could easily suggest that an independent political economy is the essential condition for cultural autonomy. Without doubt, the stronger a political economy is, the greater the chances for autonomous cultural development. The access to material resources is an important factor in supporting a certain type of cultural expression.

In the examples cited above, however, this was an elitist cultural autonomy developed at the expense either of lower status groups in the nation or of colonial dependencies. What began as a movement for political, economic, and cultural autonomy eventually became imperialist and a synchronizing force vis-à-vis weaker groups. This type of cultural autonomy has a basic inegalitarian premise, that is, that real culture can be patronized and appreciated only by the elite. The existence of a differential access to material resources has meant a cultural autonomy for only those of a higher economic status.

If cultural expression is to contribute to the development of autonomy in a society, it must be an expression of internal equality as well as resistance to imperialist synchronizing forces. Furthermore, if it is to respect the cultural autonomy of other societies, it must also avoid the temptation that as a result of its success as an adequate cultural solution within its own national social system, it becomes an expansionist, imperialist force.

ANALYSIS OF CONTEMPORARY RESISTANCE TO CULTURAL SYNCHRONIZATION

Present-day examples of resistance to cultural synchronization are to be found in Canada, Australia, Cuba, Peru, Mozambique, Tanzania, and the People's Republic of China—countries which represent quite different political and economic conditions.

Canada and Australia are industrially developed countries; as a result of the large-scale importation of cultural goods and services by way of the transnational information industry, they are closely linked to the cultural system of the United States.

Both Cuba and Peru, although economically and culturally greatly influenced by the United States, have attempted to find their own economic and cultural paths through social revolution.

Mozambique and Tanzania have only recently emerged from their colonial past; they must realize their cultural independence in the face of strong external political and economic pressure.

Finally, the People's Republic of China has so far been reasonably successful in isolating itself from the transnational communications industry and has reached a high degree of autarchy in its public media. Nevertheless, for the remainder of this century, China will also have to maneuver carefully between the desire to preserve its own cultural system and an increased opening to external influences that are coming through international information exchange, importation of technology, and diplomatic compromises.

Canada

There is increasing concern in Canada regarding the political and economic dependency upon the United States, a concern which has been especially strong in the area of public media. The Canadian government has now passed laws designed to slow the stream of imported North American media. This is one form of opposition to the inundation of the Canadian media by North American products.

Former Canadian prime minister Lester Pearson expressed well a general feeling among Canadians when he said that he had always seen what could be called a "culture pollution" as a serious threat to the Canadian identity. One aspect of this culture pollution in Canada is the widespread distribution of North American magazines and television programs.

One of the new laws passed in 1977 is in part directed against the Canadian editions of *Time* and *Reader's Digest*. In 1977, both had an extensive circulation in Canada: *Time* (Canada) sold 570,000 copies per week, and *Reader's Digest* almost 2 million copies per month. The law also encompasses American television programs which reach Canadian homes via cable from stations in Buffalo and Bellingham, New York. The television stations are among the most lucrative in the United States. Canadian advertisers are strongly attracted to both magazines and television stations; the vast sums of advertising income which leave Canada in this form represent a loss of investment in national production capacity. The new law states that magazines must be predominantly Canadian in both ownership and content. Moreover, advertising in foreign magazines will no longer be permitted as a tax deduction. This also applies to television advertising. The law discourages Canadian advertisers from seeking time on North American television stations. It is estimated that this represents a loss of approximately US $20 million for television stations in the United States. Moreover, the Canadian Radio-Television and Telecommunication Commission has now proposed the elimination of advertising from North American programs reaching Canada via cable.

As early as 1960, the Canadian broadcasters were asked to implement a regulation stipulating that at least 55 percent of the transmission time would be spent on programs which were Canadian in content.[10] This regulation was based on an article in the broadcasting law which states that the Canadian broadcasting system must be fundamentally Canadian.[11] Despite initial protest from radio and television stations, this did indeed result in a greater number of Canadian-produced programs. The quality of these programs has also greatly increased with time. Moreover, as a result of the regulation, a Canadian light-music industry has developed. There is still the problem of defining precisely what constitutes Canadian content; there are no unequivocal answers to this. In any event, decisions regarding the contents of programs are now made by Canadians, something that in itself has proved to be an important step.

Recent years have also seen the start of a strong Canadian book industry. It was almost impossible to find Canadian books 15 years ago; now there is a proliferation of them. Similarly, there now appears to be a future for Canadian magazines, some of which have already been very successful.

The Canadian interest in maintaining an independent cultural identity becomes all the more critical with the rapid development of computer-based information technology. Canadian information policy is designed to provide its citizens access to the widest possible array of information sources without, at the same time, incurring too much dependence on computer data bank sources in the United States. Canada faces the question of how transborder information flow can be regulated in a way that guarantees the privacy of the Canadian citizen.

Canada has also taken steps to preserve its independence in the field of satellite communications. The Telsat-Canada system should enable the country to maintain a sophisticated but independent nationally based information distribution network.

Australia

The Media Are American is the title of Jeremy Tunstall's extensive study of the international media industry.[12] Australia is a clear example of his point.

The 10 largest advertising firms, 8 of which are American, have 40 percent of the national advertising production. Three-fourths of the other 227 agencies are Australian-owned, but they follow North American models closely in their advertising formats. Australian television also follows the North American model and has from the beginning been heavily dependent on programs imported from the United States. So much television advertising produced in the United States is shown on Australian television that the average viewer sees more North American commercials than does the average viewer in the United States. The production of films and phonograph records is North American in both structure and content. The computerized production of books, newspapers, and other print media as well as the associated services and software are all supplied by IBM, Control Data Corporation, and NCR. The national contribution to this industry amounts to 0.4 percent of the market.

Opposition to Americanization is still weak, but its most outspoken representatives are found among Australians in broadcasting and the film industry. In 1972, the Labor government set up a special commission, the Tariff Board, whose function was to set up regulations in support of national film production and to limit television imports.

In 1973, the commission advised setting up an Australian Film Authority to encourage the production and distribution of Australian films. It was also recommended that a film and television school be founded for the development of national expertise in this area. In addition, it was suggested that there be a legal provision stipulating a higher percentage of Australian-produced radio and television programs. As of 1 July 1973, the music programs of all radio stations must have an average of 25 percent Australian artists. These stations also have to transmit as much live music and original drama as possible. The content of television programs is controlled by a relatively complicated and controversial system of grades to ensure not only a certain level of Australian programming but also a higher level of investment in special programs, which will, in turn, create employment opportunities in the television industry. This grading system prevents attempts to meet content requirements by producing quickly manufactured cheap programs ("quota-quickies"). During the first year of the point system, national television production increased by 5 percent.

The cautious movement toward national media production paradoxically is endangered by an increasing desire to export Australian productions. Australia sees attractive markets in the English-speaking Asiatic world. The commercial and technological prerequisites for such exports, however, might conceivably reintegrate Australia into the North American international communication industry.

Cuba

Since 1959, Cuba has been working toward the development of "the new individual," "the new society," and the authentic cultural expression which all this implies. Because economic and cultural factors have remained closely related even after the revolution, this goal has usually received a low priority. Cuban cultural policy is linked with the attempt to liberate the country from a dependent capitalist economy; it is also strongly determined by foreign policy. The cultural goals are constantly influenced by the deterioration or amelioration of Cuban-Soviet relations. The dependence of Cuba on the Soviet Union is reinforced, of course, by the hostile attitude of the United States toward Cuba. The situation causes a curious tension which prevents Cuba from developing a truly autonomous, adequate cultural system, despite strong desires to do so.

The news media are probably the best example of this dependence on foreign models. The Cuban press, especially the most important daily newspaper, *Granma*, faithfully reflects Pravda journalism. *Granma,* the official organ of the Communist Party Central Committee, was once called by Castro "the symbol of our revolutionary views." The newspaper has a strong political bias in favor of the party, features a pamphleteering tone, and depends heavily on the example set by Eastern European journalists. One also finds this uncritical adoption of Eastern European views on the news and other media in the publications of the Cuban federation of journalists (UPEC). The background for this is the conviction that the media must be a weapon serving the revolution; they must contribute to the formation of the new revolutionary individual. This view has also guided the development of Cuban theater and film, although in these cultural expressions, a much higher degree of authenticity is evident.

Since the 1960s, groups have been formed in rural areas in reaction to the elite Havana theater; they seek to "develop a new theatrical language, emanating from both actors and public."[13] In the past 10 years, nine important theater groups have been founded, each with its individual identity strongly determined by the region in which it operates. An example is the Escambray group, which bases its performances on the results of extensive research concerning the problems of the local population. After gathering all the relevant research data, the playwrights begin.

When we have found an approximate form, we invite people strongly affected by the theme, such as members of the party cadre and Cuban women's federation, or people associated with organizing new cattle businesses, and so forth. Their critique can help us to clarify the play.[14]

The public plays an important role in discussing the theme both during and after the performance.

Important changes have also occurred in the Cuban film industry. The Cuban Film and Art Institute (ICAIC) was founded in 1959. This brought an end to the North American domination of film production and distribution. Privately owned film-producing companies and cinemas were nationalized. North American films circulating at that time in Cuba were expropriated. Since nationalization, making a profit was no longer the most important factor; a national film industry could now be built up with objectives such as the following:

- Using film as a medium to promote the cause of the revolution and to motivate and educate the people
- Improving the level of Cuban films as well as popular tastes

In order to reach these goals, the film institute took several significant initiatives:

- A group of Cuban party members were sent to Czechoslovakia to receive training in the Barrendow studios.
- Famous directors, such as Joris Ivens and Agnes Varda, were invited to Cuba to offer classes and to direct films.

- Coproductions with various communist countries were made, for example, with the Soviet Union, East Germany, and Czechoslovakia.
- An excellent film magazine, *Cine Cubano*, was set up.

The Cuban film is an instrument for political education and must contribute toward forming the new individual, who will live in a revolutionary society characterized by new techniques, symbols, and social patterns. "The ICAIC," said its director, Alfredo Guevare, "must deal with the problems of Cuban reality."[15] To fulfill this task, an attempt has been made to change radically the distribution, form, and content of films in Cuba.

The changes in the structure of the distribution system have been especially successful in that they have made films accessible to populations in rural areas. Prior to 1959, going to the cinema was primarily an event for the urban elite. With the aid of numerous mobile projection units (by car, boat, or mule-drawn wagon) the film institute was successful in reaching millions of Cubans through the medium of film. The mobile units show news specifically geared to revolutionary ideology, documentaries which are often directed at practical problems, and feature films.[16]

The majority of the Cuban films are documentaries with the principal aim of political education. The feature films produced by the first generation of film directors trained in the film institute from 1965 to 1967 were concerned primarily with the negative aspects of the period preceding the revolution. A new period began in 1968 during which more emphasis was placed on giving expression to the revolutionary reality. After 1971, ideological themes were more often cast in the format of entertainment. It is noteworthy that most films still treat historical themes and refrain from dealing with controversial topics. An exception is the documentary film, which gained an international reputation for frank treatment of delicate issues. Recent fiction films also have been touching on contemporary problems, such as male-female role divisions and the ambiguous sexual morality in the film *A Portrait of Terese*. Another film, *La Salacion* by M. O. Gomez, denounces the sexual taboos of the older generation; *Memorias del Subdesarrola* by T. G. Alea criticizes the indifference of many intellectuals toward the political and historical context of their country. Although the documentarists have found a modern film language, as exemplified in the original work of Santiago Alvarez, the language used in most films remains problematic. Many directors have remained the captives of the Hollywood, Moscow, and Rome examples. This may be because the revolutionary artist was molded in the prerevolutionary period and in the vicissitudes of Cuban cultural policy.[17]

At the time of the revolution, radio and television were already very important in Cuba; there were various privately owned networks which controlled over 160 radio and 27 television stations. All these were under the solid control of North American firms in cooperation with the wealthy national elite. In 1959, there were 900,000 radios and 365,000 television sets. Following the revolution, radio and television, like film, had a primarily educational function. A radio and television commission was set up by the Ministry of Education for the purpose of developing education programs: one year later, "teleclasses" were followed by approximately 200,000 Cubans. In December 1975, in an address to a Communist Party Congress, Fidel Castro summarized the changes which had taken place after 1959: "The national radio and television network was set up; services were extended to the traditional zones of silence. Communication via satellite was introduced. Programming at the service of the people has begun."[18]

In 1961, the educational function of radio and television became even more important. It was "The Year of Education," during which a massive attempt was made to eliminate illiteracy. According to the government, illiteracy dropped from 21 percent to 4 percent in that year alone. During the 1963-1964 period, when national economic policy was concerned with providing necessary support to the agricultural sector, hindered by both low productivity and labor shortages, educational broadcasts were aimed at providing agricultural technical training.

In 1971, the First National Congress on Education and Culture requested a periodic, systematic analysis of educational broadcasts. In response, a meeting of the First National Forum on Educational Television was held in May 1973. The forum's conclusions recommended that television be used as a means of spreading the pedagogical principles of the revolution and that educational television contribute more systematically to the ideological and political education of the students. These suggestions were based on the statement of the First National Congress on Education and Culture about the mass media:

Mass media are powerful tools for ideological formation. Of the mass media, radio and television are those with the deepest and widest influence among the masses. As a result . . . all cultural agencies cooperate more thoroughly in order to use radio and television as vehicles of the different cultural manifestations and achievements in their highest . . . expressions.[19]

The emphasis placed on total educational reform, which characterizes the Cuban revolution, can be seen in the attention paid to the educational uses of the media. Whereas in other Latin American countries only 6 percent to 10 percent of broadcasting time is taken up by educational programs, in Cuba it is at least 30 percent.[20]

In addition to these programs, there is ample space for news and topical discussion on Cuba and socialist countries and a wealth of information about other Third World countries. Television films are very popular, especially those from Mexico and Argentina. Soap operas are also broadcast in Cuba, but they address themselves to the social inequalities of the prerevolutionary period. Television comedies promote changes in attitudes; for example, lazy fathers who neglect their household duties are made a laughing stock. There is also popularity for such programs as Informacion Publica, in which government officials respond to questions posed by the viewers. Much attention is paid to television for children, with special programs for every day of the week.

Cuban television certainly has not solved all the problems inherent in its mandate to be an instrument of social change and development. On many occasions, the Minister of Culture Armando Hart has urged television producers to fulfill better the objectives of the media in a revolutionary context by being the vehicle through which the masses can have access to education and culture. Cuban television, whatever its shortcomings, is at least liberated from the flood of imports from the United States that characterizes the television programming in most other Latin American countries.

The Prensa Latina press agency was established on 15 June 1959, to break the international monopoly in the distribution of news. By 1960, this agency had 26 correspondents working in all Latin American countries. The economic and diplomatic blockade caused problems for Prensa Latina, so that by 1961 there remained about 10 correspondents. This situation has improved since 1970, primarily because of support from Eastern European countries. By 1978, Prensa Latina had 35 offices: 12 in Latin America, 10 in socialist countries, 7 in Western Europe, 4 in Africa and the Middle East, and 2 in Asia. At the central editorial office, 400 people are employed, 100 of whom are journalists. Apart from a news service with 250 to 300 daily reports, Prensa Latina has services for special articles, illustrated reporting, and photographic material.

In Cuba, the development of the various media has been determined to a great extent by the development of national political and economic policy. In 1961, the official position of the Cuban government was that a culture had to be created which would be available to the masses and which would help them to help themselves. The importation of French and Italian films began in early 1963 and set off a nationwide debate in the press about whether or not Frederico Fellini's film *La Dolce Vita* represented a "healthy form of relaxation for the working classes." *La Dolce Vita* was allowed to be shown; many more products of the capitalistic, decadent culture followed, especially in the 1965-1968 period when Cuba was experiencing a very tense relation with the Soviet Union. In that period, every cultural expression which could denigrate social realism represented an important political action. During this period it appeared as if Cuba's cultural independence consisted primarily of the production and importation of everything which could emphasize the break with the U.S.S.R. Extensive contacts with Western European artists and intellectuals also fitted into this framework.

All this changed drastically in 1968. The deteriorating economy drove Cuba into the arms of the Soviet Union, an action with immediate cultural consequences. A strong emphasis was placed on the need to be militantly ideological. As a result, a number of prominent Cuban film directors left for Europe. The case of the poet Herberto Padillo is characteristic of this period. Among the continued attacks on artists and intellectuals who have supposedly betrayed the revolution, there was an especially vehement criticism of Padillo in particular because of his literary work *Fuera del Juego*, which had won him an international award in 1969.

Then in 1970 the ambitiously planned sugar harvest failed; this economic disaster brought the Cubans still closer to the Soviet Union. The campaigns against all forms of cultural expression began to resemble the cultural policy of Moscow.[21] Padillo was arrested and forced to confess openly to having worked against the revolution. Revolutionary leaders, such as Carlo Franqui, who stood up for him, were officially called "spiritually colonized people" and the freedom of cultural expression termed "a mask covering a counter-revolutionary attitude."

In two famous letters published in *Le Monde* in April and May 1971, friends of the Cuban revolution, such as Sartre, De Beauvoir, Sontag, and Garcia Marquez, gave expression to their concern and rejected Stalinist cultural policy. The First National Congress on Education and Culture, which met in Havana from 23 to 30 April 1971, settled accounts with these friendly critics in a manner which was hard to misunderstand. In its concluding statement, the congress said that it rejected the claim of the pseudo-leftist middle-class intellectual mafia that it is itself the critical conscience of socialist society. In fact, the congress considered them as the carriers of a new colonialism.

In its references to the mass media, art, and literature, the congress suggested that there was no room for anything but a socialist culture which expresses itself in terms of the Marxist-Leninist ideology. Admittedly, this directed the Cuban cultural system away from cultural synchronization dependent upon the capitalist culture industry. At the same time, however, this did not lead to the realization of an authentic, adequate system relating to the Cuban reality, because Cuba remained a prisoner of international relations of dependency.

Peru

Under the leadership of the left-oriented military government that came to power in 1968, there were radical reforms in the political and economic structure in Peru. The power of the propertied classes was severely limited by various measures. In agriculture, for example, control was transferred to farmers' organizations. The fishing industry, bringing in one-third of Peru's foreign exchange, was nationalized. An important portion of banking and foreign trade was also nationalized. Worker communes were established.

A very contradictory system developed, however. While the economic basis had drastically changed, the expropriated individuals still exercised control over the production of cultural goods and services. Specifically, the communication media were controlled by foreigners or by a few wealthy Peruvian families and firms. The former owners of the fishing industry, large agricultural enterprises, and banks still controlled the national newspapers. This situation was changed on 27 July 1974 when a law was passed expropriating the media. The document stated that the public media must actively make a contribution to the development of a free and unified society wherein every person has a right to self-realization.

There were three major provisions for a new structure of media control:

- Radio and television were put under state direction.
- Private ownership of newspapers and magazines was granted for a local circulation not exceeding 20,000 copies.
- Various social groups (farmer organizations, professionals, artists, workers, etc.) were given control over the large daily newspapers, thereby creating a socialized form of participatory direction of these media.

President General Juan Velasco Alvarado described the process in the following terms: "The expropriation of an enormously powerful press, monopolized by a small group, does not mean that we transfer this power to the state. . . . In accordance with our democratic calling, the revolution transfers this power to the social organizations of the country."[22] In the question of imported programming, a regulation was adopted which stated that these could not contain anything directed against either national integrity, safety, sovereignty, and economy or good morals.

This regulation led to the banning of some foreign magazines, such as *Time*, because of a report on the border conflict between Peru and Ecuador. Various womens' magazines, such as *Cosmopolitan*, were also forbidden. The reason given was that their pages introduced North American cultural models. Moreover, the government argued that foreign currency could be more profitably used for other purposes. Also prohibited was *Sesame Street* (*Plaza Sesamo*), a television series for children. Peru was the only Latin American country to prohibit it. The Ministry of Education refused to give permission to transmit this program, specifically because it felt that it reinforced authoritarian relations. Furthermore, according to a comment from the Ministry, "the reality with which the child is confronted in this program is that of elitarianism (sic), expressive consumptionism, and thoughtlessness."[23]

Peru followed a European model for commercial television: advertisement spots are time-limited and are presented in block units. The nationalized broadcasting system was to produce at least 60 percent of the programs shown in Peru. The government was given an hour of broadcasting time each day to transmit educational and cultural programs.

The socialization of the national newspapers was the most significant Peruvian measure toward resistance to cultural synchronization.

- The social pages, with their news about high society, disappeared. They were replaced with news about unions, farmer organizations, educational groups, art, and the professions.
- The quantity of international news and the variety of viewpoints were expanded. There was a wider selection available because, in addition to news from the Associated Press, United Press International, and Reuters, the services of Tanjug, TASS, Prensa Latina, and Inter Press Service were also used.
- The range and quality of news about the Third World were increased.
- The tone set in editorial commentary tended to be anti-imperialist and anticapitalist.
- Sensational journalism relating to crime and sex disappeared.
- The number of advertisements possible in newspapers was limited. Formerly, advertisements took up 70 to 80 percent of the total space available in newspapers (similar to all other Latin American countries). The new law limited this to no more than 50 percent.
- All employees of the newspaper were given the option to contribute, should they disagree with the editorial position of the newspaper.
- The readers' right to reply was protected by the law. Formerly, it was necessary for the reader to get a court order to place a com-

plaint in the newspaper. In the new situation, in principle every reply had to be published. The chief editor was required to appear in court should he or she not agree to publish. In the event that the request was refused, the newspaper was forced to pay a substantial fine.

- In Peru, about 40 percent of the population speaks an Indian language, Quechua. The newspaper *Cronica* provided, for the first time, a daily edition in this language.

This effective opposition to Americanization of the media brought on a series of problems, which undoubtedly contributed to shortening the duration of the experiment.

In many respects, government control, regardless of the participatory role played by the various social groups, remained much too strong, particularly about personnel policy. Several polemics of critical television were forbidden after 1974. Moreover, regardless of the changed ownership structure, the daily newspaper had to function according to typically capitalist principles, such as competition and income from advertising. Fundamental errors were also made in transferring the newspapers to social groups. Rural farming organizations, for example, received control of *El Comercio*, which is primarily read in the capital city of Lima. The daily newspaper, *La Prensa*, with a rural circulation of about 50 percent, became the property of the worker communes in the city.

Still more serious was the fact that not all the social sectors to whom ownership was transferred were well organized. With the exception of farmer organizations, most spheres were not sufficiently consolidated to allow them to exercise the social power granted them. This was important, since the Peruvian revolution struggled primarily against the national elite that functioned as the vehicle for Americanization. The key concept of socialization was to counter the vested interests of the dominant social stratum.

External pressure also played a role and was exerted by the Inter-American Press Association, an organization of North and Latin American newspaper owners. They judged the measures to be undemocratic and totalitarian and in conflict with the freedom of the press.

As was noted above, the experiment was terminated in 1975 after about a one-year trial.

With the "move to the right," the economic crisis, and pressure from the United States, the social revolution in Peru was cut short. A state of emergency was declared, curfews were established, strikes were declared illegal, and rigorous action was taken against unions and newspapers. In 1976, the various nationalized sectors were returned to private ownership and social ownership of businesses became a dead letter. The deteriorating economy offered a convenient excuse for foreign intervention.

President Morales Bermudez accepted a $240 million loan from a consortium of banks led by the Citibank and the Bank of America, ostensibly "to save the revolution." Nevertheless, as Dutch correspondent Jan van der Putten observed,

The American bankers have placed conditions for this help which are tantamount to halting the revolution. Privately owned firms must again receive a central position, and inconvenient limitations placed upon foreign investors must be lifted; government spending must be reduced, and social unrest must be repressed with force.[24]

A restraint was placed on the economic and cultural revolution. "But," noted Rafael Roncagliolo, "that which was begun cannot be completely nullified and our media are, in any event, less Americanized than they were prior to 1974."[25]

Mozambique

One of the most characteristic aspects of the Mozambiquan cultural revolution is the conscious effort to take elements of the colonial period and give them a Mozambiquan personality. As was noted above, Portuguese was the symbol of Portuguese oppression; yet the use of Portuguese for *Radio Frelimo* transformed it into the language of the liberation movement.

Cultural emancipation and social revolution are closely associated; people who are close to the process of creation of cultural symbols, such as media personnel, play an important part in this revolution. In the words of Jose Luis Cobaco, the Minister for Transport and Telecommunications, "Journalists must maintain close contact with the people; they must know the needs of the people, and must inform in a simple, clear language about the reality of the people."[26]

According to President Samora Machel, the information media must be "the vanguard for the revolutionary class struggle." They must make a contribution to one of the most characteristic aspects of the Mozambiquan developmental process: the mobilization of the people. It is a complicated problem for a country which has only just been liberated from four centuries of colonialism, where more than 10 dialects are spoken and the illiteracy rate is estimated at around 95 percent. The problem was extensively discussed in 1977 during the First National Congress on Information. At the congress Machel said: "During the colonialist period, information was an instrument of cultural repression. In that period, the media presented the Mozambiquan peoples as wild, inferior beings, without consciences, without a will, without culture."[27]

The central question is then: with this past, how can the media now function differently? This is indicative of a transformation which according to Jorge Rebelo, Minister of Information, will be made more difficult by the fact that "most of the journalists come from the lower middle-class. They have not had experience with the political struggle, and still carry the traces of the methods which were used during the colonial period."[28]

To aid the creation of trained journalists, the congress decided to establish a school for journalism, information, and communication. Work was also begun toward organizing an extended network of "people's correspondents." Thousands of Mozambiquans—workers, farmers, bureaucrats—can now make their contribution via a nationalized media. This contests the notion that only journalists are in a position to make news. In order to help journalists to avoid being alienated from the working class, they must spend a short period of each year working in agricultural or industrial production.

Education plays a central part in an attempt to acquire cultural independence. "It is through education that the 'new individual' will be formed." But here, also, the problem of breaking away from the colonial past exists. It is a struggle with "those who think that we have neither a history nor a culture of our own."[29] Education is vitally important and the acquisition of qualified personnel has the highest priority. When Mozambique gained its independence in 1975, there were one mining engineer, no trained mechanics, and fewer than 20 bus drivers. Education, like health care, had been a privilege of the whites. Of the 4500 students at the University of Maputo in 1974, 500 were left by 1975.

Important reforms were made in primary and secondary education, especially in areas such as history, geography, and language. These changes were effected through continual consultations with teaching staffs. Literary education now consists of texts by President Samora Machel; the late Angolese leader Agostino Neto; and Amilcar Cabral, the murdered liberation fighter from Guinea Bissau. The Ministry of Education and Culture has the goal of making the school a platform from which the people can participate in the exercise of power.

Despite the creation of a government printing and publishing office, there remains a shortage of appropriate educational books which could replace the colonial texts. Nevertheless, the improvements made in the area of education have been significant: at the time of independence, there were 500,000 schoolchildren; by 1977 there were 1.3 million.

Art is no longer considered an elitist privilege in Mozambique. A textbook notes that throughout history the most beautiful artwork has been created by the people and it represents the expression of their thoughts. That is why art is seen as an expression of the people's will and as a guide to national development.

In the working areas of the capital city, cultural activities play an important role. At the end of each week, the inhabitants present a play. Among the themes of this people's theater are Portuguese exploitation during the colonial period and the integration of the masses into the new society. Immediately following independence from Portugal, the plays performed in the working quarters of Maputo had as their theme the peaceful coexistence of the black and white populations.

Tanzania

Tanzania has sought a solution to the problem of cultural dependency since 1961. The fundamental concepts guiding Tanzanian socialism are "ujamaa" and "self-reliance." President Nyerere himself has given an extensive interpretation of these principles in various publications. Concerning ujamaa, he writes,

The foundation, and objective, of African socialism is the extended family. The true African socialist does not look on one class of men as his brethren and another as his natural enemies. He does not form an alliance with the "brethren" for the extermination of the "non-brethren." He rather regards all men as his brethren — as members of his ever-extending family. . . . "Ujamaa," then, or "Familyhood," describes our socialism. It is opposed to capitalism, which seeks to build a happy society on the basis of the exploitation of man by man; and it is equally opposed to doctrinaire socialism which seeks to build its happy society on a philosophy of inevitable conflict between man and man.[30]

The concept of self-reliance points to the necessity of developing an independent political and economic policy. The basic principles for this self-reliant process of development were set down in the so-called Arusha Declaration, which was accepted by the governing party, TANU, in 1967.

It is stupid to rely on money as the major instrument of development when we only know too well that our country is poor. It is equally stupid, indeed it is even more stupid, for us to imagine that we shall rid ourselves of our poverty through foreign financial rather than our own financial resources.[31]

This trust in money, according to the declaration, leads to dependency and to a mistaken accent on industrial, instead of agricultural, development. The development of the nation must thus take place in accordance with the ujamaa concept. Some elements of this are: opposing excessive urbanization, living in agriculturally established communities, and the furnishing of these communities according to the principle of the extended family. Mobilizing, influencing cooperative organization, and starting a new form of education are to play key roles in the developmental process.

During the colonial period, education emphasized the values of the colonizer, provided services for him, and rested upon the principles of a capitalist society. Like many newly independent African states, Tanzania in 1961 inherited a completely inadequate educational system. The first measures taken by the new government were the elimination of all racism in education, expansion of educational facilities, and stimulation of Tanzanian culture in education (the national language, national songs and dances, African history, etc.). By introducing subject matter of importance to Tanzania, education was oriented toward the formation of a new socialist society.

Education has to foster the social goals of living together, and working together for the common good. . . . It must also prepare young people for the work they will be called upon to do in the society which exists in Tanzania — a rural society where improvement will depend largely upon the efforts of people in agriculture and village development.[32]

Nyerere admits that these aims have certainly not yet been reached. In his view, education is still too elitist; there is as yet no real connection with social reality; education still breeds the idea that knowledge can only come from books and educated instructors. Moreover, it keeps too many young people away from more productive work. Nevertheless, steps are being taken to correct some of these problems through radical organizational changes in the educational system.

The public media also have a very important educational task; but the persistence of the colonial past presents a problem here as well. The models are Anglo-American; the broadcasting and other infrastructures are underdeveloped; professional personnel are lacking.

The newspapers were developed on the English model. There are now 30: 7 daily newspapers (4 in Dar es Salaam and 3 in Zanzibar) with a circulation of 61,000 and 23 weekly (or irregularly) appearing newspapers with a circulation of 213,000 copies. This is a total circulation of 274,000 for a population of approximately 14 million, an average of one newspaper per 50 inhabitants.[33] This is in contrast to a developed country such as the Netherlands, for example, where the ratio is one newspaper for every three persons.

In 1961, there were only three Tanzanians trained as journalists. This is slowly improving, as some get training in African universities, such as the University of Nairobi in Kenya.[34] Like Mozambique, Tanzania is also attempting to establish a news-gathering system through nonprofessionals. Villagers are encouraged to contribute information about local activities and events that touch on their daily lives. The distribution of newspapers is also a serious problem, owing to irregular postal services and slow train and bus services.

Illiteracy is a further problem, which makes radio more important than newspapers. There are three nationalized radio networks which transmit a combined 165 hours a week: a national program in Swahili, an English program, and a program in Swahili with advertising. Approximately 17 percent of the transmission time is spent on educational programs. As much as possible, the subject matter of programs deals with events in Tanzania; each program is expected to contribute to the national political development. There are an estimated 150,000 radios in use in the country, about 11 per 1000 inhabitants.

Film is also beginning to be an important medium; 5 million tickets are sold each year from 36 cinemas. Rural areas have some access to films through mobile projection units. Much of the film material is produced in Tanzania. With the aid of government subsidies, a large number of news and documentary films have been made in Tanzania in recent years by the Tanzania Film Unit.

Up to this point, Tanzania has resisted the pressures to introduce television. The government does not feel that the country is ready for television, primarily because only an urban elite could make use of it. Moreover, there would be an almost total dependence on imports of foreign programs.

Tanzania has instead chosen to introduce a video system which will serve primarily the rural areas. A program begun in 1972 and entitled *Tanzania Year 16* (named after the sixteenth birthday of the official ruling party, TANU) proposed to train villages in the use of video equipment. Such equipment is used for horizontal communication between ujamaa villages and between the villages and government in Dar es Salaam. In a number of cases, this appears to be an effective, easy, and inexpensive communication medium, through which an important contribution can be made to social development and political consciousness. *Tanzania Year 16* is an important beginning in the development of an indigenous communication infrastructure; by using a minimum of imported technology, there is less danger of a dependent media system.

In recent years, however, as Tanzania becomes increasingly dependent on foreign economic assistance, the strategy of self-reliant development is seriously threatened. In 1980, more than 50 percent of the government budget was based on foreign aid. Although in 1979 an agreement with the International Monetary Fund was refused because of conditions that were judged contrary to Tanzanian policies of social and economic development, in 1980 Tanzania was forced to sign an agreement. Tanzania's present economic crisis has been influenced by a number of factors, such as the conflict with Uganda under Amin and adverse climatic conditions.

An observation by René Dumont, however, is also important; this well-known author of *False Start in Africa* addresses the false start of the Tanzanian experiment. In Dumont's opinion, ujamaa was imposed from the top without sufficient involvement from the base of society. The most critical factor for social development in Tanzania is the 90 percent of the population which lives in the rural areas and which contributes about 50 percent of the national income. Many of the peasant farmers have never been convinced that the socialist experiment was necessary.[35] Whether or not Tanzania can sustain its policy of cultural autonomy depends very much on its solving the present crisis.

The People's Republic of China

The origins of the modern press, radio, film, and other information media in China can be traced back to Western, largely North American, influences. The first newspapers were established by North American and European missionaries and businessmen.

For years, the only international news agencies channeling information to and from China were *Time* and Reuters.[36] Many Chinese magazines began as imitations of *Time*. The film industry developed under the influence of Hollywood. The first Chinese filmmakers, trained primarily in Western Europe or North America, produced a large number of feature films in the 1920s and 1930s, but these were only Chinese versions of the North American western. Despite these attempts to establish a national film industry, in 1929, 90 percent of the films came from the United States; by 1937, 85 percent of the films were still being imported. Chinese radio also began as a close imitation of the North American commercial model.[37]

Since 1960, China has had a very strong policy concerning cultural autonomy. After a long history of media importation, media content is now nationally produced; an information structure has been developed which has given access to the media to millions of Chinese. In spite of a scarcity of material resources, all rural villages are reached by the creative use of some medium: films, posters, placards, or loudspeaker systems. This nationwide information network is also made possible by the powerful governmental structure of China.

The national policy of Chinese cultural independence found unexpected support in the almost complete embargo on commercial and cultural contacts which the United States established during the Korean War. When the Soviet Union turned its back on the Chinese shortly thereafter, the People's Republic was able to dedicate itself to its own development in relative isolation, independent of foreign influence.

Not all the Western influences disappeared immediately. During the 1960s, comic strips read by millions of adults and children continued to follow North American models; films still had the stamp of Hollywood.[38] Schoolbooks still contained material reminiscent of China's feudal and capitalist past; in education, knowledge was still considered an elitist possession to be derived from books and teaching authorities. Many radio programs and feature films concerned with traditional themes are scarcely touched by political content.

The cultural revolution of the 1960s was directed against these lingering elements of a past influenced by the West. The central question guiding the revolution was how China was to leave definitely the capitalist path to follow a socialist one. According to Mao and his supporters, this required that economic and cultural production be guided by a policy of decentralization, mass participation, selective development, and motivation to serve the common good. The guidelines formulated during the cultural revolution by Chou en Lai on 1 May 1966 stated: "We must forcefully bring the proletarian ideology to the fore and must banish middle-class ideals in all cultural areas."[39]

The relative merits of the cultural revolution in the 1960s have been widely questioned and debated. However, the cultural revolution did direct the media toward serving the interests of the rural and working class population. In Maoist thinking, the media were not necessarily supposed to serve the interests of the "whole people"; those who promoted the latter policy, such as Liu Shao-chi, were seen as reactionaries trying to end the class struggle. Media content was to be based upon the everyday reality of the needs of Chinese development, for example, upon the functions of the barefoot doctors. Worker and farmer communities were encouraged to develop their own artistic forms, based upon their personal experiences. At the Kwanchow film studios, producers were urged first to live and work with farmers and workers and then, in cooperation with them, to develop themes for films. Many feature films were adaptations of well-known revolutionary Chinese people's operas. Efforts were made to reach more people with the aid of mobile projection units traveling from village to village.[40]

The cultural philosophy of Chairman Mao gave direction to both the newspapers and the broadcasting system: "Our literature and art exist totally for the benefit of the masses; they are created for the benefit of the workers, farmers and soldiers in order to be used by the workers, farmers and soldiers." Thus, newspapers and the broadcasting system were to be at the service of the proletariat. As Mao defined it, the task of newspapermen was to "educate the masses, to enable the masses to know their interests, their own tasks and the Party's general and specific policies."[41] To that end, the *Daily News of the People*, with an estimated circulation of 4 million, began a network of people's correspondents who sent in 500 to 600 reports daily. These were reviewed, selected, and edited by a central editing office.

The radio stations invited farmers and workers to produce programs. Chinese radio places heavy emphasis on news programs, with up to 50 percent of the broadcasting time occupied by various forms of news reports. In addition, there are information and educational programs, as well as music reflecting revolutionary themes. The Chinese radio has also introduced a type of "wire broadcasting" consisting of a network of loudspeakers reaching approximately 100 million villagers. Courses are offered through these same channels. The estimated number of radios exceeds 15 million.

Television, too, has a system of people's correspondents. The Cantonese television station, for example, has an extensive network of non-professional television producers who fill approximately one-third of the broadcasting time. Television programming time is divided as follows: 40 percent literature and art, 30 percent documentaries, 20 percent news, and 10 percent children's programs. Most of the material is produced in China, with some programs imported from North Korea, Vietnam, and Romania; nothing is imported from the West.

The 600,000 television sets are primarily the communal property of factories and communes; groups of 25 to 100 view them.

The cultural policy of the "hundred flowers" was originally introduced by Mao in 1957. In Mao's view, "the policy of allowing a hundred flowers to bloom simultaneously and one hundred schools to express themselves is a policy promoting the development of art and the advancement of science, an endeavor to promote the flowering of our national socialistic culture."[42]

For a period, emphasis on the relatively pluralistic cultural policy of the hundred flowers waned. After the arrest of the "band of four," however, this philosophy reemerged and initiated a cultural renaissance. On the one hand, interest in classical Chinese art forms is being stimulated on a grand scale. Chinese operas and ballads have been revived; traditional wandering minstrels have once again appeared in villages and cities. On the other hand, China has once more opened the door to Western cultural expression; Chopin, Beethoven, Mozart, Shakespeare, Balzac, Tolstoy, and Heine are no longer forbidden.

The question posed by the cultural revolution comes to the fore again: Which hundred flowers must blossom in order to permit the development of the socialist individual? The recent developments arouse the fear that the flowers could be largely Western imports. The four modernizations in agriculture, industry, defense, and science, already planned under Mao, are now being carried out with considerable foreign assistance and technology. The door to cultural synchronization could very well be opened wide with the introduction of United States and British television series, advertising by foreign transnational corporations, McDonald's hamburgers, Intercontinental hotels, and the symbol of North American influence—the scattered Coke bottles. As *Variety* reports:

Under a hurriedly written pact approved by Carter and Teng, the Chinese have officially and enthusiastically opened their doors to the entire range of American cultural forms, including professional arts groups and cultural organizations, news and public information organizations, radio and television know-how, production and distribution of films, disks and other audio-visual materials, and sports.[43]

As Vietnamese scholar Tran van Dinh comments, "It is no longer the 'capitalist road' the late chairman Mao worried about; it is the capitalist Trojan horse Vice-Premier Deng Tsiao-ping has invited into the heart of China itself."[44]

RESISTANCE: SUCCESSES AND FAILURES

The case studies given above show both success and failure in the effort to resist the process of cultural synchronization. There is no case where all the conditions for bringing about a total cultural autonomy are fulfilled. It is clear that stronger economies, such as those in industrialized countries of Canada and Australia, are in an advantageous position vis-à-vis foreign dominance. But their inability to respond adequately to their internal cultural fragmentation raises serious questions. For example, is there any realistic hope for a distinct Canadian cultural identity? In the case of Peru, economic dependence combined with foreign interference supported by the internal ruling class may seriously obstruct the path toward an autonomous culture. Cuba also faces the problem of foreign dependence, although this is counterbalanced in part by a strong move toward mass participation in the cultural system. In Mozambique, a wrecked economic infrastructure is slowing down the development of cultural autonomy, but probably only temporarily. The emphasis on popular participation is strong and contributes to self-consciousness. In the view of Samora Machel, "People have to liberate themselves if the thing (transformation) is to be real."[45]

Much will depend on the restraints imposed by foreign powers. In the analysis of this chapter, the case of Tanzania reveals a clear policy and advantageous conditions for an autonomous cultural development. There is a selective combination of the traditional and the modern, a positive self-image, an effort to create decentralized information structures and, until recently, relatively little foreign interference. But Tanzania's economy has many weaknesses, so a tendency toward external dependence increases and may seriously impede cultural autonomy.

The People's Republic of China has had many of the conditions for success in achieving cultural autonomy: economic self-reliance, a mass popular movement, and very little foreign influence. In the present drive for modernization, China is running the risk of succumbing to greater dependence in its politics and economy as it opens the door to foreign interference. It still remains to be seen how much cultural autonomy will remain under such conditions.

REFERENCES

1. *Declaration by the Heads of State of the Non-aligned Countries,* Algeria, 1973.
2. The term compunication has been proposed by the Harvard University program in information technologies and public policy.
3. Euclides Quandt de Oliveira, *A televisao como meio de comunicacao de masa,* Brasilia, Government Publishing, 1974, p. 46.
4. In the Dutch daily *De Volkskrant,* 11 December 1977, p. 20.
5. Ibid.
6. *The Wretched of the Earth,* Baltimore, Penguin, 1967, p. 187.
7. Ibid., p. 188.
8. Frantz Fanon, *A Dying Colonialism,* Baltimore, Penguin, 1970, chap. 1.
9. Fanon, *Wretched,* p. 199.
10. *Board of Broadcast Governors Announcement Regarding Radio and Television Broadcast Regulations,* Ottawa, Canada, 18 November 1959.
11. *Canadian Broadcasting Act,* Ottawa, Canada, 1958.
12. Jeremy Tunstall, *The Media Are American,* New York, Columbia University Press, 1977. See also Myles Breen, "Severing the American Connection: Down Under," *Journal of Communication,* vol. 25, no. 2, 1975, pp. 183-186. One of nine articles in the Form of Cultural Dependency symposium.
13. Rense Royaards, "Theater in dienst van de Cubaanse revolutie," *De Volkskrant,* 1 July 1977, p. 37.
14. Ibid.
15. A. R. Hernandez, "Filmmaking and Politics," in Cees J. Hamelink, *The Corporate Village,* Rome, IDOC International, 1977, p. 194.
16. Ibid., p. 197.
17. See Maurice Halperin, "Culture and Revolution," in R. Radosh (ed.), *The New Cuba,* New York, Morrow, 1976.
18. J. Werthein, *Educational Television and the Use of the Mass Media for Education in Cuba,* Stanford, Calif., Stanford University Press, 1976, p. 7.
19. *Cuba '71, I Congreso Nacional de Educacion y Cultura,* Havana, Cuba, 1971, p. 21.
20. Werthein, *Educational Television,* pp. 1-6.
21. Halperin, "Culture and Revolution."

22. *Libertad de expresion y libertad de prensa,* official address, Lima, Peru, June 1975.
23. Samuel Perez Barreto, *El caso Plaza Sesamo en el Peru,* Lima, Peru, Instituto Nacional de Cultura, 1973.
24. *De Volkskrant,* 9 August 1976, p. 5.
25. During the revolutionary period, Rafael Roncagliolo was president of the Peruvian union of journalists. Private correspondence.
26. Interviewed in *Cuadernos del Tercer Mundo,* January 1978.
27. Samora Machel, "Opening Speech, First National Congress on Information, Maputo, 1977," *Cuadernos del Tercer Mundo,* January 1978.
28. In a speech at the same congress of note 27.
29. Samora Machel, interviewed in *Cuadernos del Tercer Mundo,* January 1978.
30. Julius Nyerere, "Ujamaa: The Basis of African Socialism," in J. Nyerere (ed.), *Ujamaa, Essays on Socialism,* London, Oxford University Press, 1970, pp. 11-12.
31. Nyerere, "The Arusha Declaration, February 1967," in *Ujamaa,* pp. 13-17.
32. Nyerere, "Education for Self-reliance," in *Ujamaa,* p. 52.
33. *World Communications,* Paris, UNESCO, 1975, p. 118.
34. There is another training course for journalists at the Publicity Media Institute of the Nyegezi Social Training Centre.
35. Rev. ed., London, Andre Deutsch, 1969.
36. Tunstall, *The Media Are American,* pp. 182-194.
37. Ibid., p. 195.
38. T. W. Robinson, *The Cultural Revolution in China,* Berkeley, University of California Press, 1971, p. 93.
39. Dallas W. Smythe, "Mass Communications and Cultural Revolution: The Experience of China," in George Gerbner et al. (eds.), *Communications Technology and Social Policy,* New York, Wiley, 1973, pp. 441-465.
40. Mao Tse Tung, "Talks at the Yenan Forum on Literature and Arts," in Mao Tse Tung, *Selected Works of Mao Tse Tung,* Peking, Foreign Languages Press, 1961-1965.
41. Mao Tse Tung, *On the Correct Handling of Contradictions among the People,* Peking, Foreign Languages Press, 1957.
42. Ibid.
43. 7 February 1979, p. 1.
44. "The Third World and 1979 WARC," unpublished paper, 1979.
45. Interviewed in *Cuadernos del Tercer Mundo,* January 1978.

3

Resistance to Cultural Synchronization: The International Discussion

It is clear from the discussion in the preceding chapter that the public media play a major role in attempts to resist cultural synchronization. The various examples show how the media purvey North American influence but also serve an essential function in the process of national cultural emancipation. The root of this tension lies in the duplex nature of communication processes themselves: synchronous, aimed at synchronization, consensus, and centralization; and diachronous, aimed at diversity, independence, and decentralization. All post-World War II international debates about communication and culture revolve about this tension.

On the one hand, international communication is geared toward synchronization of large audiences with a cultural system of gatekeepers (synchronic). On the other hand, international communication is expected to encourage diversity of autonomous cultural systems (diachronic).

Those who control the infrastructures of international communication defend their domination by appealing to the principle of a free flow of information; whereas those who defend the need for diversity and autonomy in the world's cultural systems continually attempt to qualify that principle.

Even the United States Commission for UNESCO grappled with this tension in their initial formulation of the free-flow principle. Their 1947 report to the secretary of state recommended:

The American Delegation (to UNESCO) should advance and support proposals for the removal of obstacles to the free flow of information. . . . The Commission . . . [believes] . . . that the organization should concern itself with the *quality* of international communication through the mass media and should give serious study to the means by which the mass media may be of more positive and creative service to the cause of international understanding.[1]

Meanwhile, the first session of the General Assembly of the United Nations in 1946 had already asked the Economic and Social Council to convene a conference about "the rights, obligations and practices which should be included in the concept of the freedom of information."[2]

The UNESCO constitution, adopted in 1945, itself reflects the tension. It accepted the principle of a free exchange of ideas and knowledge, but it also stressed the need to develop and use the means of communication toward a mutual understanding among nations and to create an increased factual knowledge of each other. Article 19 of the Universal Declaration of Human Rights embodies freedom of information as a fundamental right; Article 28 calls for the existence of an international order in which the rights of the individual can be fully realized.

Twenty years later in 1966 the General Assembly of the United Nations unanimously accepted the International Covenant on Civil and Political Rights. This came into operation in 1976 and was ratified by 45 countries in 1978. Article 19 of the covenant acknowledges the freedom of information; paragraph 13 adds that the exercise of this right carries with it "special duties and responsibilities" and may "be subject to certain restrictions."

Article 20 states the restrictions: "Any war propaganda shall be prohibited by law. . . . Any advocacy of national, racial or religious hatred that constitutes incitement to discrimination, hostility or violence shall be prohibited by law."[3]

These documents illustrate the effort to qualify total informational freedom with social responsibility. The need for such qualification became even more urgent with the introduction of the satellite in international information traffic. The specific cause of the urgency was the capability of direct transmission of television programs through the satellite to individual receivers in other countries. The 1972 UNESCO Declaration on the Use of Communication Satellites stated: "It is necessary that states, taking into account the principle of freedom of information, reach or promote prior agreements concerning direct satellite broadcasting to the population of countries other than the country of origin of the transmission."[4]

The tension presents itself in the UNESCO concern for communications between nations. Although UNESCO strongly endorses the principle of an unobstructed flow of information, it also urges the development of a "national communication policy," especially in Third World countries. In UNESCO's definition, communication policies are "sets of principles and norms established to guide the behavior of communication systems."[5]

In the UNESCO debates since 1972, the principle of the free flow of information has been qualified by the addition that the flow must also be "balanced." UNESCO developed a program to promote a "free and balanced information flow" and encouraged the director general to put it into effect.

The tension between freedom of information and national sovereignty characterized the 1975 Helsinki Conference on Security and Cooperation in Europe. The final part of the conference report stressed the important role played by the free flow of information: "Participating States . . . recognizing the importance of the dissemination of information from the other participating States . . . make it their aim to facilitate the freer and wider dissemination of information of all kinds."[6]

The first part, however, stressed that participating states shall respect each other's individuality: "They will also respect each other's right freely to choose and develop its political, social, economic and cultural systems."[7]

The nonaligned countries have made a most decisive contribution to this international debate by coupling their concerted effort toward a new international economic order with the necessity for a new international information order. In their 1973 meeting in Algiers, the heads of state of the nonaligned countries determined that "developing countries should take concerted action to reorganize existing communication channels which are a legacy from the colonial past."[8]

The March 1976 symposium in Tunis of nonaligned countries on the information media elaborated this initial determination. The final report of this meeting was entitled "The Emancipation of the Mass Media in Non-aligned Countries." The use of the word emancipation "reflects the fundamental interest . . . in their economic and political liberation, and is a basic factor in these countries which fight for independence, equality, progress, peace and co-operation."[9]

According to the symposium participants, emancipation should be brought about mainly through the efforts of nonaligned countries to introduce a new information order. Mutual cooperation, help, and solidarity were seen as the most essential instruments needed to achieve independence. In such a context, the symposium placed a priority on cooperation in supplying news, as well as in training journalists and in exchanging technology. In conclusion, the participants demanded that a mutual fund be established which would foster the development of the mass media in nonaligned countries.

Shortly after the Tunis conference, a meeting was held in Mexico in May 1976 under the auspices of ILET (Latin American Institute for Transnational Studies) and the Dag Hammarskjöld Foundation to discuss the role of information in the new international order. The participants of this conference consisted of journalists and researchers from both Third World and industrialized countries. In one of the final documents it is noted:

The development of a new international order in the area of information is an integral part of the endeavor to achieve a new international economic (and social) order. A just international order is a necessity for both poor nations and the industrialized world. Reaffirmation of political sovereignty and the struggle for economic liberation also extend themselves to the necessity for a new formula for the current flow of information. . . . Just as another authentic development toward international self-reliance is necessary in order to satisfy basic human needs, "another news" is necessary in order to reflect the actual developments in society. To realize this, sufficient conditions must be created which guarantee the access and the right to information, and which secure the cultural sovereignty of each society.

Accordingly, the final document states:

To this end it is important that Third World countries collectively design alternative information systems, which will remove current prejudices by presenting a more realistic picture of their situation. This is in agreement with a policy of total sovereignty over endogenous natural resources, and the realization of endogenous developmental models. With these, the cooperation between Third World countries will become a legitimate and necessary instrument for the achievement of their sovereignty in the areas of information and culture.

According to the participants, this process of change has already begun:

The nonaligned countries have already made noticeable advances in the development of alternative information channels, both within and outside the Third World. This growing political consciousness as well as the measures taken in relation to information make it possible that the following meeting of non-aligned countries (in Sri Lanka, August 1976) be called the "Bandung of Information."[10]

The conference of nonaligned countries at Bandung in April 1955 was the first international manifestation of mutual solidarity among Third World countries.

Prior to going to Sri Lanka for the Bandung Conference, the ministers of information of the nonaligned countries met at New Delhi from 8 to 13 July 1976. There the "pool" of press agencies of nonaligned countries was created. In the statutes of the pool, one finds the following among its aims: "to improve and expand mutual exchange of information" and "the dissemination of correct and factual information about non-aligned countries."[11]

The statutes of the pool were ratified in August 1976 in Colombo, Sri Lanka, by the heads of state of the nonaligned countries. On this occasion, it was stated that a new information order is as important as a new international economic order. Nevertheless, the only concrete action, apart from a number of declarations, was a decision to take steps toward more cooperation between the national press agencies of a limited number of nonaligned countries. This is, in fact, the continuation of an initiative taken on 29 January 1965 when a series of bilateral contracts were concluded between the Yugoslavian press agency Tanjug and the agencies of 17 nonaligned countries. The conferences of New Delhi and Colombo expanded this initiative and established a program which set guidelines for the mutual cooperation necessary to achieve a new information order. By the beginning of 1978, there were 32 press agencies from nonaligned countries associated with the pool; their mutual news exchange took place via five regional coordination centers: in Yugoslavia, Latin America, Tunisia, India, and Sri Lanka.

1976 has been called the year of the new information order, which is accurate inasmuch as in 1976 vigorous international discussion began in the media regarding the pros and cons of the suggested changes in the reigning international information structure. Many Western journalists interpreted these changes as a "muzzling" of the press. In this view,

A major movement appears to be under way by Third World and Latin American countries, that would restrict the free flow of news reporting in and out of these areas and eventually replace it exclusively with government-controlled information.[12]

Some went so far as to interpret the Third World initiatives as an omen of "Orwellian mind control on a continental scale."[13]

There were other opinions, however, such as that of the French newspaper *Le Monde*, which recognized that the criticism coming from the Third World was at least partially justified. *The Washington Post* commented: "It must be galling to Third World people to see their newspapers, films, TV-shows and even their comic books either providing trivia and circuses, or worse, promoting consumer and value models of slender relevance to their own societies."[14]

From 12 to 21 July 1976 the first of a series of UNESCO-sponsored intergovernmental conferences on communication policies took place in San José, Costa Rica. The conference called for a recognition "that a more balanced international circulation of information and communication is a just and necessary demand on the part of the Latin American and Caribbean countries." The participants, mainly from the Latin American and Caribbean region, observed "that the free flow of messages throughout the world should be based upon more just criteria for the exchanges between nations."[15]

In 1976, the 19th General Conference of UNESCO had on its agenda the debate on the "free and balanced flow of information." The "Tunisian resolution" pleaded for the support of initiatives in Third World countries to build their own information infrastructures. The resolution which among other things asked for financial support for the pool of nonaligned agencies was almost unanimously accepted.

THE WIDENING DEBATE ON "THE NEW INTERNATIONAL INFORMATION ORDER" FROM 1976 TO 1980

The initiatives, resolutions, and comments mentioned so far set off a discussion which continued with great intensity throughout the late 1970s. A survey of the most important meetings during this period indicates how the debate took shape.

In April 1977, UNESCO invited working journalists to discuss the international flow of information at a meeting in Florence. Some 138 journalists were involved: 90 from Western and 18 from Eastern European and 30 from Third World countries. No resolutions, decisions, or recommendations were made. There was only an exchange of ideas. One of the participants noted, "There were few results because they (the participants) were more intent on attacking each other, and became very confused when they were required to contribute solutions to the problems."[16]

Harry Lockefeer of the Dutch newspaper *De Volkskrant* concluded:

It appears, therefore, of the utmost importance, first, to set up, by all available means, organizations and training programs which will provide the Third World a means of retaliation and the possibility of participating in the world information flow; second, to organize in each country a more effective journalism directed towards the national problems. That would certainly be a contribution towards developing a new world order in the area of information.[17]

In September 1977 a very controversial meeting, the ILET seminar, took place in Amsterdam, concerned with international communication and Third World participation. Journalists, researchers, and government officials discussed two main points:

- The current state of affairs with respect to Third World participation in international communication
- Suggestions for a more participatory communication structure

In November 1977 in Tampere, Finland, the new information order was the theme of a discussion between journalists and scientists from

Eastern and Western Europe. In this symposium, organized by the University of Tampere and the International Institute for Peace of Vienna, the central concern was the possibility of international agreements to regulate the activities of transnational information industries.

In the same month, the Third International Colloquium of the International Organization of Journalists (IOJ) met in Baghdad. The discussions were primarily devoted to the political, economic, and cultural implications of the decolonization of information.

From 3 to 5 November 1977, the Italian Cinni Foundation, in cooperation with the International Press Institute and the magazine *Affari Esteri* organized a conference in Venice. Approximately 60 journalists participated in this discussion on the theme of new perspectives in north-south communication. Jean Schwoebel, chief editor of *Le Monde*, suggested that 30 important international newspapers be regularly supplied with a supplement concerning the new economic and information order.

The Seventh General Meeting of the International Peace Research Association (IPRA), held in Oaxtepec, Mexico, from 11 to 16 December 1977, also discussed the new international information order. The papers and discussions were primarily concerned with the relation between the new economic order and the need for a new world system of information distribution and access.

In 1977 and 1978, the International Press Institute (IPI) also turned its attention to the debate on the new information order and specifically addressed itself to UNESCO. The twenty-sixth annual meeting of this association of publishers and editors-in-chief held in Oslo in June 1977 passed a resolution urging all member countries of UNESCO to devote themselves to defending both the freedom of the press and the freedom of expression. The following annual meeting in March 1978 in Canberra took up the question of whether or not Western-style journalism is appropriate for the Third World. In discussing this matter, the disagreement with UNESCO emerged once again. There was a lingering fear that the UNESCO machinery wanted to push through directives which would permit government interference with the media.

During 1977, the activities of the World Press Freedom Development Committee began to take form.[18] This committee, founded by a group of North American journalists and media directors, has as one of its goals that of contributing to the training of Third World journalists. By the end of 1977, the committee had 28 subdivisions on 5 continents and was working with organizations such as the Inter-American Press Association, the Press Foundation of Asia, and the International Press Institute. These organizations furnished financial aid for training projects in Third World countries such as Kenya and Trinidad. They also began collecting old broadcasting equipment and machinery used for graphic production to be put at the disposal of Third World media. The Third World media can also appeal for assistance to the group's "manpower pool," made up of approximately 500 North American journalists, mostly retired, who are prepared to teach their colleagues in the Third World short-term courses in the tricks of the trade. The committee further decided to finance a series of seminars on international communication. The first seminar met in Cairo in April 1978, under the auspices of the Fletcher School of Law and Diplomacy at Tufts University in Medford, Massachusetts.

Apart from these private initiatives, there was some interest on the part of the government of the United States. In the later part of 1977, a report written by George Kroloff and Scott Cohen for the Committee on Foreign Relations of the Senate of the United States was circulated among various government departments and senators. In the introduction, Kroloff and Cohen note:

Whether we like it or not, there will be a "New World Information Order." It could be the driving force and the fuel for the "New World Economic Order" called for by the Less Developed Nations. The outlines of the "New World Information Order" are becoming clear. The blanks will be filled in during a series of international meetings in 1978 and 1979. These meetings, for which the United States is *totally unprepared* at this writing, could be as important as any others in this decade, because. . . they will

- significantly shape the way people and nations will relate to each other;
- be a key factor in the development of future technology; and
- affect the actions of the government of the United States.[19]

At the end of the report, the authors ask the following fundamental questions of the American government:

- How can the flow of information be increased to better all mankind without impinging upon personal privacy, proprietary data and national security?
- How can — or should — the Second and Third Worlds' desire to rigidly control information sectors of their societies be accommodated, while trying to allow free flow of information worldwide?
- How can the United States Government organize to protect our security, cultural and economic interests and also help meet the needs — and gain the cooperation — of the developing nations?[20]

In April 1978, a meeting in Stockholm was called by the UNESCO-appointed International Commission for the Study of Communication Problems.[21] Large and small press agencies and their clients and journalists' organizations discussed "the infrastructures of news collection and dissemination in the world." The Third World presented its well-known list of complaints about the functioning of large Western press agencies. The West retorted that the restrictions placed on journalists in the Third World seriously obstruct good reporting. The participants from the West nevertheless readily admitted that the Third World is at a disadvantage in terms of technical means and professional training. There were no objections to accepting suggestions for remedying this situation.

Shortly after the meeting in Stockholm the same topic was discussed in Holland by approximately 50 specialists invited by the Netherlands UNESCO commission. The purpose of this exchange was to prepare and inform the Netherlands delegation to the 29th General Conference of UNESCO in October 1978 in Paris.

During 1977 and 1978, many conferences convened which were concerned primarily with the technological and financial aspects of the international supply of information. An important related point on the agenda was the reduction of telex and telephone tariffs on information traffic between Third World countries.[22]

During conferences in Jakarta and Havana (both in April 1978), the nonaligned countries expressed their support for reinforcing the pool initiative for taking forceful action to bring about a new information order.

A highlight in the debate during this period was the 20th General Conference of UNESCO, held in Paris in November 1978. The conference received the interim report of the International Commission for the Study of Communication Problems (the MacBride Commission). A resolution was adopted that supports the establishment of "a more just and effective world communication and information order." Also adopted was the "Declaration of fundamental principles concerning the contribution of the mass media to strengthening peace and international understanding, the promotion of human rights and to countering racialism, apartheid and incitement to war."

Another important event was the combined UNESCO-Intergovernmental Bureau for Informatics (IBI) meeting held from 28 August to 6 September 1978 in Torremolinos-Malaga, Spain. It was the first Intergovernmental Conference on Strategies and Policies for Informatics (SPIN). The conference considered "that informatics is a phenomenon of global importance for mankind and that it requires the full cooperation of all countries in the implementation of coherent programs which. . . are in keeping with the requirements of the establishment of a new international economic order."[23]

Journalists and media policymakers met in a conference in Bonn from 4 to 6 December 1978. The conference "Toward a New World Information Order: Consequences for Development Policy" was organized by the Institute for International Relations and the Friedrich Ebert Foundation. Conference participants agreed that a new international information order was necessary in order to achieve a free flow and a wider and better-balanced dissemination of information throughout the world. The conference especially stressed the need for the development of horizontal information exchange between the developing countries.

Finally, in 1978, the 33rd Session of the United Nations General Assembly adopted on December 18 a resolution which "affirms the need to establish a new, more just and more effective world information and communication order, intended to strengthen international peace and understanding, based on the free circulation and wider and better balanced dissemination of information."[24]

Journalists from the nonaligned countries met for the first time in Baghdad from 21 to 24 January 1979 and prepared a final declaration in which the peoples, countries, and institutions of the nonaligned movement are reminded that "they must exert efforts to set up the basis for a new international information order to overcome the shortcomings in this field, which efforts are not permitted by imperialist circles, because they see in these the end of their domination and a blow to their control."[25]

In Kuala Lumpur, Malaysia, from 5 to 14 February 1979, UNESCO convened the Intergovernmental Conference on Communication Policies in Asia and Oceania. This was the Asian counterpart of the conference on communication policies in Latin America and the Caribbean that had taken place in San José, Costa Rica, from 12 to 21 July 1976. The conference expressed the "need to establish a new, more just and more effective world information and communication order to redress the imbalanced flow of information between the developed and the developing countries."[26] It was also recognized that it is imperative for this new order to be of "benefit to the masses of peoples in the developing countries."[27] Therefore, the assembly recommended that UNESCO and other United Nations agencies

assist in the early establishment of research and development programs designed to make available the necessary technology and expertise for the low-cost production of media equipment and materials so that the facilities of all media are available to and within the financial capacity of the average citizen of developing countries.[28]

From 3 to 8 September 1979, the nonaligned summit met in Havana, Cuba, and adopted a resolution to intensify cooperation in the field of information and the media.

The Conference considers that in order to establish the new international information order and to insure a flow of information that is not one-way, it is vital to set up national information systems and national media, to strengthen national information sources in areas of key importance for the social, economic and cultural development of each country and people and for their joint action at the international level, to train national personnel in each country with the assistance of the other members of the Non-aligned Movement and of the international community.[29]

In Tashkent, a meeting of journalists and researchers from 46 countries also took place from 3 to 8 September 1979. This seminar, sponsored by the U.S.S.R. National Commission for UNESCO, cautioned that "the free flow of information is a grossly commercial concept serving the interests of transnational corporations, especially with the development of the new communication technologies such as satellite telecommunications and computer systems."[30] The seminar concluded, among other things, that "appropriate national communication systems could only be established on the basis of endogenous social needs and efforts of the people."[31]

The general World Administrative Radio Conference (WARC) was convened in 1979 by the International Telecommunications Union (ITU) for 10 weeks in Geneva beginning September 24. Attended by delegates from 154 countries, the conference had the task of reviewing and revising the international distribution of the electromagnetic spectrum. The conference debated questions of frequency allocations for satellite transmissions, access to satellite relays, high-frequency allocations, and sensing satellites.

From 6 to 9 November 1979, a UNESCO conference involving 31 nations took place behind closed doors in Washington. United States Representative Roland Homet said about the conference:

The purpose of the meeting was to seek to define an international mechanism that could work effectively to advance shared goals of communications around the world. . . . The search for a viable international institutional communications mechanism is worthwhile and should be continued.[32]

The conference was a preparation for UNESCO's Intergovernmental Conference on Communication Development in Paris, 14 to 20 April 1980.

In many ways, 1980 marks an essential point in the New International Information Order debate. The MacBride report, from the International Commission for the Study of Communication Problems, was published and became the focus of much discussion.[33] The major arguments posed by Third World countries were increasingly accepted in the journalistic and academic worlds. The focus began to turn to discussion of how the proposals could be implemented. There was added emphasis on more participatory communication structures in developing countries.

From 4 to 22 February 1980, a workshop took place in the Institute of Social Studies in the Hague, the Netherlands, where communications researchers from the Third World developed strategies for research on Third World realities. In their report, the participants identified as a most urgent task

to break down communications structures which are characterized by monopoly control in whatever form. The inherent features of such structures, verticalism and authoritarianism, should be abolished. Faced with such features, a new international information order must imply the contrary: democratization, genuine public access and social participation.[34]

Under the auspices of the International Coalition for Development Action (ICDA), the Vienna Institute for Development (VID) and the United Nations Non-Governmental Liaison Service, a meeting was held in Geneva from 27 to 29 March 1980. The main theme was "the new world information and communication order: the role of nongovernmental organizations."[35] The discussions addressed the urgency for nongovernmental organizations to become involved in the new information order movement. Among several proposals, it was suggested that both the communications industry activities of transnational corporations and the mass media coverage of Third World issues be monitored continuously.

In Mexico City from 1 to 3 April 1980, the second consultative meeting of international and regional organizations of journalists took place. Participating organizations included the Latin American Federation of Journalists, the International Organization of Journalists, and the Catholic Union of Journalists. Their *Mexican Declaration* states that a new international information order "understood as an integral part of the New International Economic Order, is aimed at the decolonization and democratization of the field of information and communication on the basis of peaceful co-existence and with full respect for cultural identity."[36]

In April 1980, UNESCO headquarters in Paris hosted the intergovernmental conference for cooperation on activities, needs, and programs for communication development. The principal goal of the meeting was to set up a mechanism through which the development of communication infrastructures in Third World countries could be supported. The conference, emphasizing the need to establish a new international information and communication order, invited the Director General to submit to the 21st General Conference of UNESCO a project for the establishment of an International Program for the Development of Communication (IPDC).

From 5 to 7 June 1980, the Intergovernmental Coordinating Council for Information of the Non-aligned Countries held its fourth meeting in Baghdad. In a resolution on the new international information order, the meeting recommended that the new order be based on

the right of every nation to develop its own independent information system and to protect its national sovereignty and cultural identity, in particular by regulating the activities of the transnational corporations. (The meeting also stressed) the right of every nation to participate in the international exchange of information under favorable conditions in a sense of equality, justice and mutual advantage.[37]

It was emphasized that the new information order is intended to contribute to the establishment of the new international economic order.

The UNESCO-sponsored meeting on communication policies in Africa took place in Yaoundé, Cameroon, from 22 to 31 July 1980. The representatives of the African member states of UNESCO adopted the *Yaoundé Declaration* in which they argued strongly for the decolonization of communication structures. They identified as a priority "the establishment and expansion of infrastructures for the exchange of information and cultural life, and for the endogenous production of all kinds of messages and cultural products."[38]

During August 1980, in New York, the United Nations Committee on Information met and recommended that the Joint United Nations Information Committee (JUNIC) "should continue to promote a new world information and communication order and give more importance, in its own activities, to communication and education components and promote the inclusion of an information component in every major developed project in the United Nations system."[39]

In the same month, also in New York, a United Nations-sponsored meeting with nongovernmental organizations took place which discussed the "Agenda for the Eighties: People's Strategies for Development." Five sessions were devoted to communications issues with the new international information order as the underlying theme.

In September 1980, the first international Islamic mass media conference was held in Jakarta, Indonesia. The meeting noted that the imbalance in world reporting has created news standards that do not suit the interests of the Third World nations, including the Islamic world. The participating countries decided to set up a media council to guarantee cooperation in balancing the anti-Moslem reports in the world's mass media.

The 21st General Conference of UNESCO in Belgrade, Yugoslavia, during October 1980, was perhaps the major development. Focal points of the discussion were recommendations made by the MacBride report and by the intergovernmental meeting called by UNESCO in April (mentioned above). As a result of the latter, the UNESCO General

Conference supported the establishment of a program and a fund for the improvement of communication infrastructures in Third World countries. Following the debate on the MacBride report, a resolution on the new world information and communication order was adopted unanimously. The contents of this resolution summarize well the major issues of the New International Information Order:

Elimination of the imbalances and inequalities which characterize the present situation; respect for each people's cultural identity and the right of each nation to inform the world public about its interests, its aspirations and its social and cultural values; respect for the right of all peoples to participate in international exchanges of information on the basis of equality, justice and mutual benefit; respect for the right of the public, of ethnic and social groups and of individuals to have access to information sources and to participate actively in the communication process.[40]

EVALUATING FIVE YEARS OF INTERNATIONAL DEBATE

The 1978 UNESCO General Conference was a turning point in the debate on the New International Information Order (NIIO), insofar as at this meeting the hostile opposition of many journalists and politicians in the First World was softened toward the introduction of NIIO. There began to be almost unanimous acceptance that Third World countries had justifiable complaints and that concessions must be made by the First World. Kaarle Nordenstreng sees this acceptance as part of a strategic design aimed at achieving "a stage of mutual accommodation in a spirit of compromise."[41]

Paving the way for this strategic design and seeming acceptance of major proposals of Third World countries at the meeting was the reformulation of the key concept underlying the debate. The original formula coined by the nonaligned movement, "the new international information order," was replaced by "a new, more just and more effective world information and communication order." It is unlikely that this is coincidental, since the formula "new international information order" always closely linked with the new economic order, posed a challenge for Western political and economic interests. It demanded nothing less than the fundamental restructuring on a global basis of international information flows and a qualitative change in the contents of those flows.

According to the interpretation of United States Ambassador John E. Reinhardt, indicated at the 1978 UNESCO General Conference, the new order would require

a more effective program of action [including American assistance], both public and private, to suitable identified centers of professional education and training in broadcasting and journalism in the developing world. . . . [It would also imply] a major effort to apply the benefits of advanced communications technology — specifically communications satellites — to economic and social needs in the rural areas of developing nations.[42]

In line with Reinhardt's statement is one of the resolutions adopted at the conference requesting the Director General

to intensify the encouragement of communications development and to hold consultations to lead to the provision of developing countries of technological and other means for promoting a free flow and a wider and better balanced exchange of information of all kinds.[43]

The new order in its reformulation seems to be acceptable because it reduces the problems of international information mainly to the transfer of professional know-how, technology, and financial resources.

Since 1978, the new order has been accepted by Western governments and rather than maintaining the former critical attitude, they now have an active desire "to shape the future course of the new world order as co-architects."[44]

The question is, of course, whose new order is it actually that is now so unanimously embraced and about to be implemented. As some United States corporations have quickly understood, the emphasis on transfer of resources can be exploited as a legitimation of Western market expansion. It is hardly coincidental that immediately after the UNESCO meeting, several large communication corporations began to introduce a new phraseology in advertising their goods and services to the Third World. For example, electronics manufacturer General Telephone & Electronics said, "One of the Third World's first needs is good communications. G.T.E. is in a unique position to help bring modern communications to these nations." As the advertisement aptly says, "it is another demonstration of how we try to be in the right place at the right time for all our markets."[45]

The new world information and communication order could very well turn out to be the world order of the transnational corporations, the corporate village, but now with international political blessing. Karl P. Sauvant observes that a similar development seems possible toward the new economic order:

With its reliance on transnational enterprises [it] is not likely to be a framework for a new and more equitable world economic order, but rather, designed to stabilize the present order and thus contain a further deterioration of the position of developing countries.[46]

The expansion of international information flows will primarily benefit the networks of large transnational industrial and financial corporations. As Herbert Schiller notes:

Increased linkages, broadened flows of information and data and, above all, installation of new communication technology, are expected to serve nicely the world business system's requirements. That they can be considered as constituting a new international information order is so much additional icing on the cake of the transnationals.[47]

The new international information order seems to follow the same route as the new international economic order. The basic framework is created by the transnational corporations. As the president of IBM's European Division, Jacques Maisonrouge, observed recently, "They [transnational corporations] have become agents of change and progress, for they are building what, for all intents and purposes, must be considered a new world economic system."[48]

It is unfortunate that despite all its positive contributions, the Report of the International Commission for the Study of Communication Problems (the MacBride Commission) has not offered a clear and perceptive definition of the new international information order. Specifically, it also did not produce the kind of conceptual framework that would make the coopting of the new order by more powerful contesting parties less likely.[49]

On the whole, this series of events brought about an impressive, albeit verbal, commotion. Little has actually been done in terms of far-reaching, concrete action which could change the existing information structure. This could be owing to three factors:

- A constantly recurring distortion in the various discussions is the identification of information and mass media with news and press. In the many declarations and resolutions, there is a strong emphasis on the press, the news, and journalists, as if they are the key actors in international communication. The crucial questions of control over economic, technological, and marketing structures in international communication are left untouched.
- In many instances, there has been no relation between the development of media technology and communication policy, partly because discussions of these issues have taken place in different contexts and involved different groups. As a result, agreements may be reached at the level of lofty, abstract principles, but there is no hope that these will be implemented, because there is no control over technological infrastructures. (There is, for example, no access to satellite frequencies.) It may also be the case that policy is formulated on the basis of the functional characteristics of media that have become obsolete as a result of rapid technical developments. For example, current

policy often treats transborder media flow and computer-based data flow as separate problems, when the two are merging into one process.
- In order to convert the present information order into a new international information order, at least three steps are needed:

  1. In most Third World countries, fundamental political changes are needed that would lead to social structures in which the informational needs of all social groups can be taken into consideration. This applies not only to the Third World but also to more industrially developed Western and socialist countries.
  2. Governments of Western countries will have to be prepared to control more strictly the activities of transnational corporations, including corporations of the communications industry.
  3. Governments of the socialist countries will have to be willing to cooperate with decisive changes in the economic and technological infrastructure of international communication.

In all three of these steps, the problem is essentially political. Profound changes in present national and international communication policies and an overcoming of political resistance to their implementation is not going to be achieved simply by more technology or better training. The real issues are at the level of the distribution of social power.

So far, most of the discussion has been an attempt to formulate policies in quite abstract terms. The political establishments that discuss these matters at international conferences generally have not taken significant measures to implement the proposals outlined above.

So far, some of the more noteworthy concrete developments toward a new information order have been the *News Pool of the Non-aligned Countries,* a few *regional initiatives,* and the increasingly important Third World agency, *Inter Press Service.* These are at least important models that suggest practical alternatives to the present information order.

REGIONAL INITIATIVES

One regional initiative that should be mentioned is the Caribbean News Agency (CANA), which was established in 1975 with the aid of UNESCO. After an initial cooperation period with Reuters, CANA became an independent and private undertaking. Within one year, the

5000 word-per-day capacity was expanded to 24,000 words and the number of subscribers doubled. The news flow both between Caribbean countries and between the Caribbean and other regions thus sharply increased as a result of CANA.

Africa represents another region making a strong effort to create a positive, concerted action. In the past, there have been many efforts toward creating an African press agency. In March 1978, the Kenyan Undersecretary Elisha Godana announced that there were once again plans for a Pan African news agency to counterbalance the Western control of the news flow. This would involve cooperation among 49 African and Arab countries and was intended to be operational by the end of 1979.

In April 1979, the information ministers of the Organization of African Unity member states agreed to the establishment of the Pan African News Agency (PAFNA). At their meeting in Addis Ababa, they decided that the agency would become a clearing house for the distribution of materials prepared by national news agencies of African countries. A major task of PAFNA would be the correction of the image of Africa, distorted by the biased and negative reporting of foreign press agencies.

Besides the African initiatives, there is the continually improving cooperation between Arab and Asian television news services. In 1973, the Arab States Broadcasting Union established its own regional news exchange system. It was at first limited to Syria, Lebanon, Jordan, Egypt, and the Sudan but has been expanded to an exchange of daily television news among all Arab countries and with the European systems Eurovision and Intervision.

The Asian Broadcasting Union, later renamed the Asia Pacific Broadcasting Union, decided in January 1977, after a series of conferences, to begin a number of trial projects for the exchange of television news in the various regions of Asia. In Southeast Asia, an exchange was begun between Malaysia, Singapore, Indonesia, and New Zealand with the coordinating center in Kuala Lumpur.

In 1976, there were 6241 news items exchanged between the Arab and Asian regional news services, of which 37 percent were of Arab origin, compared with only 12 percent in 1975.

Most recently, in November 1981, the Fifth General Assembly of the Organization of Asian News Agencies (OANA) celebrated the inauguration of the Asia-Pacific News Network (ANN). This network became operational from 1 January 1982 and is seen as an important complement to the large international news agencies. National agencies from the region are transmitting their news during some 15 minutes each day through distribution centers in Tokyo, Manila, Jakarta, New Delhi, and Moscow.

INTER PRESS SERVICE

Apart from the large, long-established news agencies, such as Reuters, United Press International, Associated Press, and Agence France Presse, there is only one alternative international news service which represents a specifically Third World perspective, Inter Press Service (IPS).[50] At present, IPS has a staff of approximately 200 permanently employed journalists and approximately 60 offices throughout the world; IPS functions as a collective of journalists who determine both policy and appointments. Profits are not paid out; they are reinvested in the agency to make further expansion possible.

IPS was founded by a group of Latin American and European journalists who shared convictions regarding the problems of development and social change in Latin America and who felt that existing news services were not providing adequate information in either Europe or Latin America. About 40 of these journalists, all involved with the small Roman Press Agency, met in 1964 in Eicholz, West Germany, to establish IPS.

In the initial phase of IPS, between 1964 and 1968, a primary purpose was to stimulate a dialog between Latin America and Europe, especially between like-minded political groups and governments. In this early period, IPS instituted a special service of interchange of embassy information bulletins in a number of Latin American countries; the first contracts were in Argentina, Peru, and Chile. This provided a steady source of income, sustaining other more innovative kinds of news services.

However, as politics moved to the right in Latin America with a growing number of military governments, IPS found it increasingly difficult to sign contracts with governments. From 1964 to 1968 there was also the period of the miscarriage of the Alliance for Progress launched by President Kennedy. The small group of IPS journalists with their reformist ideas met with a steadily diminishing response, and IPS almost disappeared from sight. From 1968 to 1971, survival became the most important goal. The number of agencies in both Latin America and Europe was reduced; the Latin American central office was moved from Santiago, Chile to Buenos Aires; but the headquarters in Rome was maintained.

In 1971, IPS decided to redefine the role of the agency. As the failure of reform in Latin America became increasingly clear, IPS saw that their journalistic activities would have significance only if they contributed to eliminating the relations that kept Latin America and other Third World countries in perpetual dependency. The guiding philosophy of IPS became the "decolonization of information."[51] IPS then moved to deemphasize its Latin American focus and expanded to

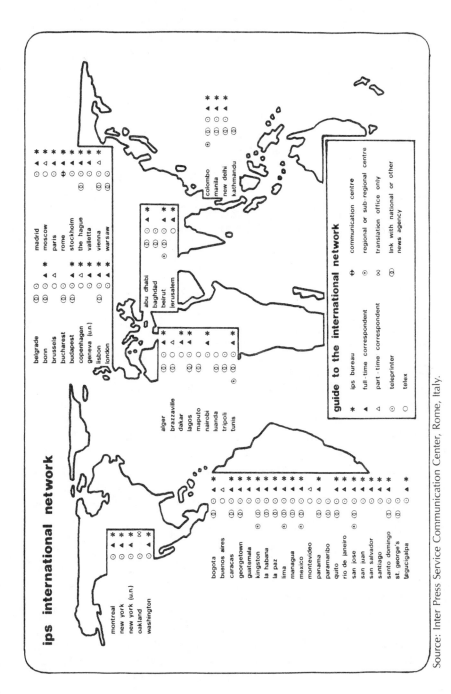

Source: Inter Press Service Communication Center, Rome, Italy.

Figure 1   The Distribution of the Offices of Inter Press Service

become a specialized agency providing a "new" type of information between Third World countries and the more developed countries.

With a more coherent information policy, IPS was in a position to extend rapidly its services worldwide. A series of important contracts was established with national news services in Africa, Asia, and the Middle East which shared similar objectives, for example, with the Tanjug agency of Yugoslavia, INA of Iraq, and ARNA of Libya. Through Tanjug, IPS later established links with the News Pool of Non-aligned Countries. Already as early as 1971, the Non-aligned Countries requested IPS to carry out the official reporting of their conference in Peru.

In the late 1970s, together with groups such as the News Pool of Non-aligned Countries IPS became one of the leading promoters of the New International Information Order. IPS also entered into a series of special agreements with international organizations concerned with development and was selected by the United Nations Development Program (UNDP) to carry out a feasibility study for an information network throughout the Third World.[52]

IPS places its journalists, wire services, and other technical infrastructures at the service of press agencies in Third World countries in order to contribute to a horizontal two-way traffic in the international information exchange. The purpose is to promote an accurate understanding of the cultural, political, and economic realities of the Third World. IPS emphasizes information on the problems which the great powers cause in the Third World, the ties which Third World countries have developed among themselves, and the relations between Third World countries and industrial countries.

With this information, IPS directs itself to a market in both the Third World and the industrial countries. In the Third World, its function is primarily one of creating solidarity and integration, especially strengthening the network of information channels by filling the vacuum left by the existing channels. In the industrial countries, IPS supplements the information offered by the large international news agencies, which generally tend to emphasize spot news; the sensational and curious phenomenon of far-off countries; and the superficial, stereotyped symbols of allegedly backward peoples. IPS material is meant to assist its readers in understanding the deeper causes of problems in developing countries. IPS does not intend to compete directly with the existing agencies, but rather to offer an alternative news service with more emphasis on analysis, interpretation, and description of social developments in their historical and cultural context. IPS tries to provide a more systematic and continued coverage of issues and nonelitist view of events then do the other news sources. IPS specializes in accurate, informed, and in-depth news about the development process and problems in Third World countries.[53]

Although IPS still has a strong base in Latin America and the two major centers of the IPS network are Panama and Rome, it is steadily opening new agencies throughout the Third World. IPS provides daily bulletins in Spanish (35,000 words per day), English (20,000 words per day), Portuguese (5000 words per day), and German (6000 words per day) and expects to begin a French-language service soon. IPS now uses satellite transmission to distribute its information within Latin America, Europe, and other regions.

In addition to its basic news services, IPS offers a wide range of more specialized services. For example, IPS has a joint project with UNESCO for the production of women's feature services, focusing on the role of women in the development process in Latin America and in Africa. IPS is also producing a daily bulletin for the "Group of 77" missions at United Nations offices in New York and Geneva.

Clients represent about 400 newspapers, governments, and university institutions in Latin America, Western Europe, Eastern Europe (Yugoslavia, Romania and Hungary), and other regions of the world. Through its expanding network of agreements with national press agencies, most Third World countries have access to the IPS service. In North America, IPS cooperates with a U.S.-based associate, Interlink Press Service, which uses IPS information services and communication networks and transmits information to media, research and action groups, and academic institutions in the U.S.

A good deal of IPS material is used by the press in Mexico, especially by the newspapers *El Dia* and *El Universal*. Other Latin American countries where regular IPS reports are published are Peru (through *El Comercio*), Colombia (*El Frente*), Argentina (*La Opinion en Hoy*), and Bolivia (*Presencia*). In Europe, IPS reports are published principally in Italy (*La Republica*), Yugoslavia, Portugal (*Diario de Lisboa*), and England (*The Guardian* and *The Newsline*).

IPS also provides a series of weekly specialized bulletins on agriculture, petroleum, the church in Latin America, economic analyses, defense, and the environment.

Compared with the big four international news agencies, IPS is still relatively small, but it is presently the strongest and most economically viable alternative to the conventional news agencies. It provides a highly professional alternative source of news. More important, while the debate continues on the distortions in the existing news services, IPS is actively defining a new type of information format.

However, the journalistic establishment and the large international news agencies meet the challenge of IPS with silence. Publications such as Rosemary Righter's *Whose News: Politics, The Press and the Third World*[54] attack efforts of many Third World nations to set up their own agencies and introduce a different news format, but totally ignore IPS, which is widely respected by journalists and international agencies for offering a most competent service and filling a vacuum in the very services that are defended.

The challenge presented by IPS is mainly owing to the new conception of information that it offers. This is important because a new order is constituted not by a single substitution of new information channels but by a new content in the information.

With its more accurate and in-depth news of developing countries, IPS also calls into question the gatekeeping practices in the conventional information channels that have come to be generally accepted. The IPS alternative exposes the value judgments underlying many of the current information services and suggests that these services may have to be completely revamped if they are to maintain their credibility in both journalistic and lay circles.

Agencies such as IPS also pose a challenge to existing news agencies in that they are offering a special service attractive to many Third World media and in line with the communication policies of many developing countries. By creating a network of information channels between Third World countries that does not have to pass through New York, London, or Paris, these agencies are respecting the demand for cultural autonomy that is certain to be ever stronger in the new nations. As agencies such as IPS improve and expand their technical infrastructure, they are likely to be increasingly competitive with the dominant First World-oriented services.

THE NEW INTERNATIONAL INFORMATION ORDER

One of the most striking characteristics of the international discussions and initiatives related to a new international information order is the one-sided attention paid to the phenomenon of so-called news. The concept of information is thus restricted to only one of its aspects; the whole problem of information processing, as well as its contribution to cultural synchronization, is approached from this one aspect.

As a result, a serious misrepresentation of the problem occurs:

- In the total international information exchange, news represents a relatively minor part.
- In the process of cultural synchronization, news plays a much less important role than do many other information processes, such as education, advertising, and computer traffic.

- By concentrating on news, the transnational industrial structure of the international supply of information can easily be overlooked; attention focuses on one small part of the information industry, while the hard core of the problem lies with those businesses, such as the advertising industry, which have a far more vital interest in opposing the profound changes in a new information order.
- As a result, there is a danger that the problem will be reduced to a question of more transfer of western technology and know-how and a greater access to Third World countries for Western journalists.
- Thus, the discussion is taken out of the context of the international dependency relations and the necessity for a fundamental reordering of those relations.

The merit of all the international conferences listed above is that they help to make it increasingly clear which elements constitute the opposition to a new international information order, however that is interpreted. The elements can be summarized in the following ten points:

1. There is no acceptance of a relation between a new international economic order and a new international information order. This is, in effect, a denial that the problem is one of politico-economic structure.
2. The core of the problem is considered to be in the Third World itself (for example, the paucity of technical knowledge and resources). There is a willingness to solve these problems, but under Western conditions.
3. One requirement is that the Western interpretation of the concept of free flow of information be maintained, which is deemed to be threatened by Third World initiatives.
4. It is proposed that the initiatives are authoritarian by nature, and under the pretext of aiding the Third World are, in fact, an attempt to undermine Western liberties.
5. The Western notion of professionalism must become the model to be followed, the presupposition still being that ideologically neutral techniques are involved.
6. The definition of information as a social good and of information dissemination as a public service must be discarded, because it is a detriment to the individual freedom of the information entrepreneur and his employees.
7. Proposals for reformation coming from Third World countries are seen as being necessarily influenced by governments and are therefore deemed unacceptable.

8. In connection with this, the suggestion to restructure the international order is seen as being inspired by totalitarian communist regimes.
9. A new order of information processes implies that rights and privileges of information industries should be defined in international agreements. This is rejected as an infringement of the freedom of information. The powerful corporations and professional groups which distribute information prefer to be equated with all other citizens in the marketplace of society so that there will be no special regulations of their functions.
10. When a new order requests a fundamental democratization of the information media and widespread participation in making national information policy, the opposition argues that the influence of social groups on media content represents an infringement of the freedom of media content.

In order to continue profitable discussions regarding the new international information order, it is necessary to balance out the conflict between a number of concepts, which have come to the fore during the debates, specifically:

- Freedom versus sovereignty
- Responsibility versus autonomy
- Freedom of the press versus freedom of information
- The professional guru versus social participation
- Information as social criticism versus information as an instrument of social development

Freedom versus Sovereignty

When the first and third "baskets" of the final protocol of the 1975 Helsinki Conference are compared, it becomes clear that a conflict exists between the concepts "freedom" and "sovereignty." This is related to the heated international debate between proponents of the "free-flow" doctrine and the defenders of national cultural sovereignty. It is fruitless to continue pretending that these standpoints are absolutes to be applied everywhere just as they are stated. The principles need not necessarily be mutually exclusive, since in practice, every country limits whatever might possibly detract from its sovereignty. The example of the United States is the most convincing, because it is there that freedom of information is so fanatically defended. During the UNESCO debate concerning the direct transmission of television programs from one country to another via satellite, it was determined that the receiving country must first give permission for the entry of the programs. The United States was the *only* country opposed to this guideline. Nevertheless, the Federal Communications Commission in the United States has placed severe restrictions on the entry of foreign broadcasting into its territory. An attempt, for example, by China or the Soviet Union to transmit television directly to the American public would no doubt meet with restrictions and would, perhaps, even be blocked completely. Or if a Canadian television company, for example, should wish to transmit pornographic programs to the United States via satellite, the government in Washington would immediately forbid it. In other words, the United States wants to have the right to prior consent but has no wish to extend this right to others.

Responsibility versus Autonomy

Characteristically, professional groups defend the autonomy of their practice vis-à-vis other groups and society as a whole. Professional communicators, maintaining a tradition of freedom of expression, are especially sensitive to outside interference. Based on this desire for autonomy, there is often a strong resistance to accepting codes which link professional practice to certain social criteria. But it is precisely the need to guarantee to citizens that freedom of expression and the importance of the professional in realizing this freedom that require that the profession be practiced within a framework of social responsibility. Arguing for regulation of international information exchange supports rather than infringes on professional autonomy. This is certainly the case when the professional group itself decides on such norms and accepts them as binding. The professional norms will not only establish responsibility toward society, however, but will also provide protection against intervention by government or powerful corporate industrial clients.

Freedom of the Press versus Freedom of Information

Press freedom as opposed to freedom of information leads directly to consideration of the conflict between the freedom of the mass media and the freedom of information based on the citizen's right to know. In the existing information structures—both capitalist and socialist systems—the freedom of the media generally exceeds that of the citizen. This is important, because in almost every country, the freedom of access to information of the citizen is considered a fundamental constitutional right. The United States offers a good example of a society in which the freedom of the media is deduced from the general freedom of information. In the United States Constitution, the right of the citizen to knowledge and to the expression of his or her opinion is fundamental; the media, in exercising its freedom, must honor this right. The freedom to access to information for the citizen is thus also a guarantee against the possibility that the media may use this freedom against the ordinary citizen. Each society must design its own mechanisms for adequately handling this potential conflict.

The Professional Guru versus Social Participation

Whenever the freedom of the media is in the service of the citizen's freedom of access to information, the communicator is no longer the guru, but becomes a part of the society. In connection with this, Jean Schwoebel of *Le Monde* has correctly observed that you cannot leave information dissemination to journalists alone. This is similar to the conviction that religious faith is too important to be left only to theologians. In the debate on the new information order, the emphasis is placed upon the social nature of information. Whoever reads pure state control into this does not see that it is essential for a society that decisions on information policy, as well as on information dissemination, be a matter of participation and cooperation between different groups in society, including professional communicators. The Peruvian experiment described above, with all its shortcomings, indicates how different social sectors can participate in making information policy and even in directing the media.

Information as Social Criticism versus Information as an Instrument of Social Development

Equally pointless is the conflict between those who see the public media as principally a form of social criticism (the tradition of the press as fourth estate, investigative reporting, etc.) and those who see the media as simply conforming instruments of national development planning. If actual media practice in most countries is examined closely, it is evident that something of both of these ideal types may be found. In countries where the freedom of information philosophy is an important criterion for information policies, information is still expected to support broad national goals and, in practice, the media tend to support the dominant political and economic interests. Research on media institutions in Western industrial countries provides abundant evidence of powerful social controls influencing the supposedly completely free media.

On the other hand, in most Third World countries there is at least some professional commitment to public criticism in the media, although this may be expressed differently than in an Anglo-American context. In many cases, given the need to motivate a nation toward relatively rapid development in the face of immense problems, it seems reasonable to expect of journalists an ethical commitment to support these efforts. Often the balance of factors in a development process is so delicate that the expenditure of national energies in continuous rancorous debate (especially when ethnic and tribal divisions lie just below the surface) is a luxury that cannot easily be afforded.

In both developed and developing nations, far more could be done to encourage the media to engage critically and constructively in a social emancipation process which challenges the concentration of social power. In both cases, the danger is that information will be treated in commercial and narrowly professional terms without any relation to the deeper social and political processes in those countries.

THE BASIS FOR A NEW INTERNATIONAL INFORMATION ORDER: COHERENT AND UNIFIED NATIONAL INFORMATION POLICIES

In Chapter 1 the process of cultural synchronization was described and analyzed. In Chapter 2 and in this chapter, various forms of resistance to the synchronization process have been pointed out at the national, regional, and international level. The most prominent manifestation of this resistance is represented in the movement to develop a new international information order.

In the debates surrounding this proposal, both the proponents and opponents tend to reduce the concept of information to one category—news. The discussion is thus diverted into a relatively superficial analysis of problems (for example, whether journalists in Third World countries are adequately trained or whether existing international news agencies have the right percentage of Third World news). As more compromises are made, the focus has tended to drift away from profound changes in the international information order to emphasis on reform of the present system. At times the debate has bogged down into arguments based on slogans whose meaning is often unclear and which are unrelated to real media practice. The many conferences and meetings have not been very fruitful, because the problem has been removed from its context, namely, the existing political and economic dependency relations and the destruction of the cultural autonomy of many nations.

What has often been lacking in the discussions is a clear focus on the causes of this threat to cultural autonomy and a search for a *coherent* set of objectives that can guide national and international policy formulation. Given the different cultural, political, and historical backgrounds of the various nations and regions participating in the debate, different actors obviously tend to emphasize one aspect more than another. What is needed is a *unifying* policy that gets to the basic causes of cultural synchronization and, at the same time, outlines a comprehensive, internally consistent framework for national information planning.

The following chapter analyzes the concept of "cultural dissociation" and proposes this as a basis for planning more adequate national information systems in the Third World.

REFERENCES

1. *Report of the United States Commission for UNESCO to the Secretary of State,* 1947.
2. United Nations, General Assembly, First Session, December 1946, *Resolution 59.*
3. United Nations, General Assembly, 17th Session, 1966, *International Covenant on Civil and Political Rights.*
4. *Declaration of Guiding Principles on the Use of Satellite Broadcasting for the Free Flow of Information, Spread of Education and Greater Cultural Exchange,* Article IX, Paris, UNESCO, 1972.
5. *Report of the Experts on Communication and Planning,* COM/MD/24, Paris, UNESCO, 1972, p. 8. See also *Towards Realistic Communication Policies,* UNESCO paper 74, 1976, pp. 32-38.
6. *Final Act of the Conference on Security and Cooperation in Europe, Helsinki, 1955,* Paris, UNESCO, 1955.
7. Ibid.
8. *Declaration by the Heads of State of the Non-aligned Countries,* Algeria, 1973.
9. "The Emancipation of the Mass Media," Final Report of the Symposium of Non-aligned Countries, Tunis, May 1976, in Cees J. Hamelink, *The Corporate Village,* Rome, IDOC, 1977, pp. 177-182.
10. *La informacion en el nuevo orden internacional,* Mexico, Instituto Latinoamericano de Estudios Transnacionales (ILET), 1977. This documents the ILET meeting.
11. Hamelink, *Village,* p. 183.
12. *International Herald Tribune,* 29 July 1976.
13. *Newsweek,* 6 September 1976.
14. S. S. Rosenfeld, "Behind the UNESCO Flap," *Washington Post,* 12 November 1976.
15. Intergovernmental Conference on Communication Policies in Latin America and the Caribbean, *Final Report,* COM/MD/38, Paris, UNESCO, 1976, p. 25. For a critical evaluation, see O. Capriles, "Acciones y reacciones en San Jose: el debate de las comunicaciones en La UNESCO," in A. R. Eldredge (ed.), *El desafio juridico de la comunicacion internacional,* Mexico City, Nueva Imagen, 1979, pp. 81-124.
16. Harry Lockefeer, *De Volkskrant,* 23 April 1977.
17. Ibid.
18. Among those to take the initiative were: Jack Howard, chairman, Scripps-Howard Newspapers; Herbert Schlosser, president, National Broadcasting

Company; Leonard Goldenson, chairman, American Broadcasting Company; Richard Salant, president, Columbia Broadcasting System News.

19. *The New World Information Order,* United States Senate Committee on Foreign Relations, November 1977, p. 1.

20. Ibid., p. 24.

21. This 16-member commission, under the chairmanship of diplomat Sean MacBride, was the outcome of the Nairobi general conference, which assigned to UNESCO's secretariat the task "to undertake a review of the totality of the problems of communication in modern society." The mandate for the commission can be found in Sean MacBride et al., *Many Voices, One World: Communication and Society Today and Tomorrow,* Paris, UNESCO, 1980, p. 295.

22. Some were: Ministerial Conference of the Press Agencies Pool, July 1977; Coordination Committee of the Press Agencies Pool, January 1977; Asian News Agencies, January 1977; International Expert Committee for Telecommunication of Non-aligned Countries, May 1977.

23. *Analytical Report of the Results of the SPIN Conference,* SPIN Document 212, Rome, UNESO/Intergovernmental Bureau for Informatics (IBI), 1978, pp. 49-60. Recommendations adopted at the SPIN conference.

24. United Nations, General Assembly, 33rd Session, 18 December 1978, *Resolution 33/115.*

25. *Final Statement of the First Meeting of Journalists of Non-aligned Countries,* Baghdad, Iraq, 24 January 1979.

26. Intergovernmental Conference on Communication Policies in Latin America and the Caribbean, *Final Report,* COM/MD/42, Paris, UNESCO, 1979, p. 35.

27. Ibid., p. 50.

28. Ibid.

29. *Resolution of the Non-aligned Summit on Cooperation in the Field of Information,* Havana, Cuba, September 1979.

30. U.S.S.R. National Commission for UNESCO, *International Seminar of Journalists in Tashkent,* Moscow, Novosti Press Agency, 1980, pp. 130-140.

31. Ibid.

32. *Editor & Publisher,* 17 November 1979, p. 48.

33. MacBride, *Many Voices, One World.*

34. Cees J. Hamelink (ed.), *Communications Research in Third World Realities,* The Hague, Institute of Social Studies, 1980, p. 32.

35. *The Role of Non-governmental Organizations—Strategies for Development Communications in the North,* ICDA/VID/United Nations Non-governmental Liaison Service, Workshop on the New World Information and Communication Order, Geneva, 27-29 March 1980.

36. *Mexico Declaration,* Consultative Meeting among International and Regional Organizations of Journalists, Mexico City, 1-3 April 1980.

37. *Resolution Adopted at the Fourth Meeting,* Intergovernmental Coordinating Council for Information of Non-aligned Countries, Baghdad, Iraq, 5-7 June 1980.

38. Intergovernmental Conference on Communication Policies in Africa, Yaoundé, Cameroon, 22-31 July 1980, *Final Report*, CC/MD/46, Paris, UNESCO, 1981, pp. 23-26.
39. *World Broadcast News*, September 1980, p. 6.
40. *Resolution*, 21st General Conference of UNESCO, Belgrade, September-October 1980.
41. "Struggle around the New International Information Order," partially published as "Behind the Semantics—A Strategic Design," *Journal of Communication*, vol. 29, no. 2, 1979, pp. 195-198.
42. *General Policy Statement by United States Ambassador John E. Reinhardt*, 20th General Conference of UNESCO, Paris, 1978.
43. *Resolution*, 20th General Conference, Paris, 1978. This resolution was prepared jointly by Australia, France, Sri Lanka, Tunisia, the United States of America, and Venezuela.
44. John E. Reinhardt, "Towards an Acceptable Concept of the New World Information Order," paper presented at the United States-Japan symposium, Boston, Mass., 11 October 1979, p. 5.
45. The General Telephone and Electronics advertisement appeared in various newspapers in the United States during December 1978.
46. "The Role of Transnational Enterprises in the Establishment of the New International Economic Order: A Critical Review," in E. Lazlo and J. A. Lozoya (eds.), *Strategies for the New International Economic Order*, New York, Pergamon, 1979.
47. *Who Knows: Information in the Age of Fortune 500*, Norwood, N.J., Ablex, 1981, p. 16.
48. *The New Internationalist*, March 1980, p. 22.
49. For a critical evaluation of the MacBride report, see Cees J. Hamelink (ed.), *Communication in the Eighties: A Reader on the MacBride Report*, Rome, IDOC International, 1980.
50. See Renny Hokelin, "Alternative News: A Case Study on IPS," in Tapio Varis et al., *International News and the New Information Order*, Tampere, Finland, University of Tampere, 1977; Phil Harris, "Bridging the Gap: Inter Press Service in the Service of the Third World," in *News Dependence*, report for UNESCO, Paris, UNESCO, November 1977, chap. 8; Jacques van Aernsbergen et al., *Inter Press Service: News from the Third World*, Nijmegen, The Netherlands, Catholic University, 1979.
51. Roberto Savio and Phil Harris, "Inter Press Service: The NIIO in Practice," *Media Development*, vol. 27, no. 4, 1980, p. 38.
52. Ibid., p. 42.
53. Ibid., pp. 38-39.
54. New York, Times Books; London, Burnett Books, 1978.

4

National Information Policies: A Plea for Dissociation

F rom a review of the still inchoate and scattered efforts to resist dependency in the field of international information, it is evident that we must search for a more adequate response to cultural synchronization. The key question in this chapter is concerned with how the Third World can develop *effective* policies to maintain and strengthen its cultural autonomy.

In the international discussions that have evolved over the past decade, the question of information and cultural autonomy is intimately linked with the need for a new international economic order. The first part of this chapter examines more closely this relation.

THE NEW INTERNATIONAL ECONOMIC ORDER AND THE NEW INTERNATIONAL INFORMATION ORDER

> Sometimes education can start announcing the new society. But in order that the announcement becomes concrete, it is absolutely necessary for the infrastructure of society to change.
>
> **Mario Cabral,**
> **Minister of Education,**
> **Guinea Bissau**

Two concepts have increasingly become the major focuses of international debates and negotiations: the new international economic order and the new international information order.

In September 1975, the Dag Hammarskjöld Third World Journalists' Seminar (which met during the 7th Special Session of the United Nations General Assembly) stated:

For the new international economic order to emerge, peoples of both industrialized and Third World countries must be given the opportunity of understanding that they share a common interest in creating international conditions that will permit another development of societies in all parts of the world.[1]

The Rio report, coordinated by Nobel laureate Jan Tinbergen insisted that

the widening of the capacity to inform must be viewed as an essential component of attempts to create a new international order and, as such, the monopolistic and discriminatory practices inherent in current international information dissemination must be deemed as one of the worst, though subtle, characteristics of the present system.[2]

In 1976, the summit meeting of the nonaligned countries in Colombo, Sri Lanka, declared: "A new international order in the field of information and mass communications is as vital as a new international economic order."[3] In these positions bringing about a new information order is seen as an essential contribution to the advent of a new economic order. As former Venezuelan President Carlos Andrés Peréz stated succinctly, "There will never be a new economic international order without the liberation of the information order."[4]

There can be little doubt, indeed, that reshaping the international order will demand a fundamental replacement of the stereotyped, alienating, and discriminatory sets of ideas that current communications structures perpetuate. The transformation of present global inequalities and injustices requires another type of information, "one which will fight preconceived ideas, ignorance and alienation, and facilitate the conscientization of citizens to ensure their control over decision-making."[5]

A basic element in the process of restructuring international relations will be international public opinion. As the Rio report rightly claims:

Public opinion in the industrialized countries will not have real access to full information on the Third World, its demands, aspirations and needs, until such time as information and communication patterns are liberated from the market-oriented sensationalism and news presentations which characterize them at present and until they are consciously stripped of ethnocentric prejudices.[6]

This demands that the present information order move "from an unidirectional to a multidirectional structure, from an ethnocentric to a culturally pluralistic and multidimensional perspective, from the receiver's passivity to active participation, from dominant transnational influences to a multinational balance."[7]

International information processes will have to be liberated from their "monopolistic and discriminatory practices":

- To present a realistic picture of existing economic power relations
- To contribute to the insight that dependency relations ought to disappear
- To make cultural autonomy possible

However, the problem is that these international information processes are an integral part of the dependency relations that determine the economic, political, and cultural organization of the current international order. The international relations stem from the development of Western territorial and economic expansion that was consolidated in the nineteenth century with the internationalization of industrial capitalism. In conjunction with this expansion, Western techniques, symbols, and social patterns were exported to the colonized territories [8]

As indicated before, it is only in the second half of the twentieth century that this occurs on such a massive scale and, at the same time, so subtly that one can describe it as transnational cultural synchronization. Moreover, despite the fact that the new nations have achieved independence as sovereign states, they are still confronted with an international order controlled by their former colonial metropolitan powers.

Thus, drastic changes in the current international order are necessary if a new information order is to come about. The two aspects of a new international order are linked together in a dialectical way, so that not only will fundamental economic changes have to support changes in the information order but changes in the informational structures will also support basic economic transformation. To paraphrase Mario Cabral, international information can start announcing the new international order; but for that announcement to become concrete, it is absolutely necessary that the economic order change.

These dialectics make it meaningful and possible to develop proposals for the new international information order based on the perspective of the new international economic order. The cohesive element in this relation is the conception of information as a "resource."[9]

On the world market, information—in all of its ramifications—is a resource that is collected, processed, and marketed, just like all other economic commodities. As with other resources, the control over its production and distribution is grossly maldistributed among the nations of the world. Yet information as a resource offers opportunities to dependent countries which are more readily accessible than are other resources, such as mineral or agricultural resources. Unlike other resources, information can be collected, processed, and marketed many times over. The national exploitation of the information resource can, therefore, be embarked upon without the immediate nationalization of foreign industries and a complicated protective legislation, which may take years to design and many more to be implemented.

Moreover, the exploitation of the resource information can be done with more indigenous capabilities and less transfer of capital and technology than is the case with many other resources.

Information as a national resource is a liberating force in the economic and cultural emancipation of a country, if its exploitation is guided by the principles upon which a new ordering of international economic relations should be based.

THE NEW INTERNATIONAL ECONOMIC ORDER

The international economic order that emerged after World War II was designed in its general dimensions by the 1943-1944 Bretton Woods Conferences held in New Hampshire in the United States. With almost no involvement of the Third World, the basis was established for such institutions as the International Monetary Fund, the World Bank, and the General Agreement on Trade and Tariffs (GATT). These institutions offered a development model to the Third World in which the growth of developing countries would be intimately linked with the existing colonial metropolis-satellite structure. The model projected a type of industrial development in the Third World nations that would be strongly oriented toward markets in the metropolitan countries. It was assumed that with the growth of metropolitan markets, the demand for goods produced in developing countries would also vastly increase. Many of the developing countries would have a very weak industrial base, but by their using the comparative advantage of cheap labor, a certain type of labor-intensive industry could be established which would allow them some participation in the international trade of manufactured goods.

Instead of forcefully encouraging receiving countries to build up their own infrastructure of finance and technology, new industries would be established with the support of large financial and technological transfers from the metropolis, especially through the emerging economic structure of the transnational corporation. Industrially less-developed countries would thus become better integrated into the world economy, and the increased employment that the new industrialization offered would at least lead to higher national incomes and, supposedly, a more equal distribution of national income.

After World War II and especially since the mid-1960s, many developing countries indeed experienced an industrialization process, but one that had a strong external dependence on the markets of the wealthy, industrially advanced countries. Such export-linked production has generally become part of the vertically integrated manufacturing structure of the transnational corporations.

However, this model did not generate the kinds of improved economic conditions in the satellite countries that were expected. Whereas during the 1960s the market economies of the metropolitan countries enjoyed an unprecedented growth, the countries with a dependent industrialization experienced an increasing economic lag, and the international development efforts that were highly touted in such plans as the First United Nations Development Decade met with almost total failure.

Serious questions were thus raised about the validity of a model that was still based essentially on a colonial structure; and its fundamental assumptions increasingly came under fire from political leaders as well as economists in academic circles. In the late 1960s and early 1970s the questioning brought about proposals for alternative development models based on concepts such as self-reliance, basic needs, and a new international economic order.

Since 1974, the basic principles of a new international economic order have been formulated in a number of declarations and programs of action. Most were proposed by Third World countries and have met with approval from a majority in the international community.[10]

The key principles are:

- The sovereignty and equality of states
- The full and effective participation of all states in international decision making
- The right of all states to adopt appropriate economic, political, and cultural systems
- The full, permanent sovereignty over national resources
- The right to regulate the activities of foreign entities, such as transnational corporations, in concurrence with national goals and priorities
- The right to formulate a model of autonomous development geared toward the basic needs of the population
- The right to pursue progressive social transformation that enables the full participation of the population in the development process

With these principles, some basic assumptions of the present economic order have been questioned in a fundamental way. These assumptions are:

- The present economic system is fundamentally sound and the crisis that we are faced with is only of a temporary nature.
- The present economic order is in the interest of both the industrialized and the Third World countries.
- Poor countries will be able to develop as long as rich countries remain rich and let their affluence trickle down to the poor.
- The model of development applied in the rich countries is also the best possible model for the poor countries.

Confronting these assumptions, the new economic order claims:

- Since the beginning of the 1970s, the economic crisis is the result of the fundamental breakdown of traditional economic mechanisms.
- The present economic order is incompatible with the Third World ambition of total emancipation; since this order is rooted in colonial exploitation, it can operate only against the interest of the Third World.
- The trickle-down effect does not work in the relation between rich and poor countries; moreover, the development of the international community has to depend on the development of *all* its members, who decide on an equal footing about economic developments.
- Development in Third World countries cannot be an imitation of Western models; the purpose is not to catch up with the rich countries. The development in the Third World that must take place will respect national sovereignty and limit the influence of decisions taken elsewhere.

In the proposals for the new international economic order, the crucial concept is *sovereignty*. But one should not confound sovereignty with a concept of nationalism as we know it from European history. It had an extraterritorial meaning that could often cause armed conflicts as the national proprietary rights were extended to include other countries. In the new economic order, sovereignty pertains to the national territory itself; it implies protection of whatever national resources a nation has. The core of the concept of sovereignty is that of making self-reliant development possible. The new economic order in this respect differs from earlier development strategies that often stressed the integration of Third World countries into the international economic system. Opposing the integration into an international system that continues economic dependence, the new economic order designs an independent development as the basis of an international system in which states participate on an equal footing.

Such a reordering implies that Third World countries must decide autonomously about their own social arrangements. A self-reliant development does require decisive social transformations. This points to a close connection between the international and the national orders. Changes in the international order cannot be achieved without related changes in the national order. The international order has to create the necessary space for national sovereignty; the national order has to translate this space into effective policy.

Despite the wide discussion of these principles for a new international economic order, especially from 1974 onward, there has still been relatively little improvement achieved in the economic relations of the Third World with the advanced industrial countries. Much of this may be owing to the rigidity of present economic structures. But one must also question the shortcomings and inconsistencies implicit in many of the proposals for a new international economic order.

A fundamental premise of many of these proposals is a claim of sovereign control over a nation's resources. But this control does not automatically make a country less dependent if in its international relations it does not have the power to bargain with its national resources. Bargaining strength presupposes building some form of countervailing power by developing countries. Such power would make it possible for developing countries to enter into international trade and other negotiations with reasonable chances of equitable exchange. Apart from the oil producers' cartel, no effective bargaining power has been created among less-developed countries during the past decade.

Underlying this failure to build countervailing power is a crucial inconsistency in the proposals: despite their demand for autonomous development at the level of policy discussions, these countries remain more oriented toward the metropolis than toward each other. As a consequence, they have concentrated very little on formulating common, mutually complementing national policies and have not directed much attention toward strengthening horizontal linkages among themselves.

This inconsistency between the demand for national autonomy and the continued linkage with current international relations is particularly evident in the emphasis on a strategy of interdependence, which is so central to much of the debate on the new international economic order.

In the present structure of international political-economic relations, interdependence is virtually equated with a hierarchical dependency relation between powerful and powerless countries. In such a process of interaction between parties of unequal strength, it is illusory to think that through a joint effort the weaker nations will develop an economic system which responds primarily to the needs of its own people. In the interchange, nations with a more developed technological base will instead tend to hold the margin of advantage, and the more

powerful the nation, the more it will exploit the interdependent relation to its own benefit. Furthermore, the greater the volume of
economic interchange between unequal parties, the greater will be the
disadvantages of the powerless.

Some suggest that in trade relations satellite and metropolitan countries are mutually dependent, but such a concept is very deceptive if one
considers the technological advantage of the latter. Can one really argue
that the leading industrialized countries are dependent upon the Third
World for their development? What is the significance of the often pro-
claimed dependence of the industrialized nations if they can substitute
the Third World's cheap labor force with automated machinery, if they
increasingly protect their markets against products from Third World
countries and if, as a final recourse, they are ready to secure their access
to Third World resources militarily with rapid deployment forces?

The thesis of interdependence has found strong support from the
protagonists of the new realism. This strand of development thinking
has gained strength in the member countries of the Organization for
Economic Cooperation and Development (OECD), especially since
1978. It emphasizes that aid to developing countries will increase their
potential for buying products on metropolitan markets and that such
improved trading relations will be in the enlightened self-interest of the
industrialized countries.

Aid, however, tends to flow mainly to the so-called middle-income
countries. According to the World Development Report of the World
Bank in 1981, the 36 poorest countries receive only 37 percent of the
total development aid.

In reality, the aid-trade model tends to focus the interdependent
relations upon countries that are the most promising trading partners,
integrating them more firmly into the existing international economic
order. This inevitably further undermines the chance for autonomous
development in the Third World.

In the current international order, the concept of interdependence
represents an unequal relation between sovereign but *dependent* states.
The *new* international economic order, however, would have to
establish a relation between states that is based on sovereignty and
equality for all. A concept more appropriate for this relation would be
interindependence.

On the basis of the principles and concepts elaborated so far, the
new international economic order could be defined in the following
way:

An organization of international economic relations in which states, by
developing their economic system in an autonomous way and with complete

sovereign control of resources, fully and effectively participate as independent members of the international community.

THE THESIS OF DIETER SENGHAAS

In an important contribution to the international debate on development, Dieter Senghaas has proposed the thesis of "dissociation."[11] He claims that dissociation from the metropolis-centered economy offers the only way toward an adequate development process in Third World countries. Such a development process would have to be achieved through a variety of measures, such as:

- An increase in agricultural productivity
- An increase of non-export-oriented industrial production of mass consumption goods, rather than fancy, luxury goods for middle and upper classes
- Establishment of facilities that create independent means of production
- Development of adequate infrastructures for collective needs
- Full exploitation of available human and natural resources

The present asymmetrically structured international economy makes such a development process impossible. Third World countries generally have at their disposal most of the resources that they need for their development. Their chances of developing their economies cooperatively are optimal, however, only if they dissociate themselves from the conditions that govern the structure of the world market. At present, the most powerful parties active in the market determine these conditions primarily in terms of *their own needs*. Only dissociation will make the satisfaction of Third World basic needs possible. If they do not choose this option, Third World countries will become only more dependent.

Dissociation should be an essential component in the proposals for a new international economic order. Without dissociation, all the proposals—for enlarged transfer of technology, finances, and other resources; for the improvement of trade conditions and better regulation of markets for raw materials—will make the satellite countries even more dependent.

Dissociation and Self-Reliance

Dissociation, or "delinking," as it is sometimes referred to, does not necessarily find support in all Third World countries at present. Resistance is particularly strong where the governing elite has a strong cultural and political orientation toward the metropolitan countries. Consequently, in these countries industrialization tends to follow the metropolitan model, and trade relations are largely oriented toward the metropolitan export markets.

But without dissociation, action programs for a new economic order are merely "new wine in old vessels." As Senghaas puts it, the new order could easily end up being a mere conflict over the distribution of resources between the metropolis and the Third World social classes that have been integrated into the international economy.[12] It is precisely these social classes, the political and economic elites and the privileged classes of the Third World, who will be inclined to choose according to their own interests, that is, against dissociation and for integration.

However, the integrationists have built up their close linkages with the metropolitan economies largely on the basis of the rapid growth and affluence of the North Atlantic nations in the 1960s. Since the mid-1970s, economic growth in these countries has been slowing down, and without the prospect of limitless growth of markets, the association may no longer be so attractive to the dependent countries.

The decision on a national policy of dissociation may be a direct challenge to the interests of a traditional governing elite. It often implies profound structural changes and a transition to a new political leadership with a broad popular democratic base within a country.

Where social structures are rigid and power is largely concentrated in the hands of the leading elite, the risks are high. On the one hand, the political leadership emerging from the radical social transformation through which dissociation is achieved may maintain itself only at the cost of strong internal controls. On the other hand, as the case of Chile indicates, where dissociation is attempted through a careful process of social change, it can be subverted by combined internal and external pressures. In order to be successful, dissociation has to combine resistance to external synchronization with internal equality (see p. 33).

It is important to note that the dissociation proposed by Senghaas is not identical with autarchy.[13] International exchange will continue to take place, but on conditions that were described above as inter-independence. This implies that in international cultural, economic, and political exchanges, the sovereign states will select what promotes self-reliant development. Indeed, the concept of self-reliance is central to the strategy of dissociation.

This principle of self-reliant development has been increasingly stressed in the past decade. An important example of this thinking is the statement of the Cocoyoc declaration drawn up by participants in the 1974 symposium on "Patterns of Resource Use, Environment and Development Strategies." In this statement, self-reliance could "imply a temporary detachment from the present economic system; it is impossible to develop self-reliance through full participation in a system that perpetuates economic dependence."

Self-reliance can be defined as the domestic determination of development objectives and the self-confident use of local resources. Self-reliance represents an alternative development model that moves away from emphasis on linkage with the metropolitan countries and that concentrates on the exploitation of indigenous resources for the benefit of the indigenous population. Self-reliance as a strategy "requires, in its collective dimension, that the political, economic and socio-cultural structures created to link colonies to metropolitan countries (in a status of dependence) be altered to link developing countries to each other."[14]

With self-reliance as the objective, dissociation means the conscious choice against the delusory offer of integration in an international order which appears to respond to all the interests of the developing countries, but which, in fact, represents almost exclusively the interests of the powerful. Dissociation demands a questioning of all international relations of interdependence between metropolitan and satellite countries and developing a strategy of relations in terms of the concept of interindependence. It also demands the abandoning or reformulation of exogenously defined objectives, priorities, and cultural images and ideals. Taken in a strict sense, dissociation means the development of a distinct personality—a political, economic, and cultural personality which is not imitative. As Fanon wrote during the Algerian liberation struggle, "We today can do everything, so long as we do not imitate Europe, so long as we are not obsessed by the desire to catch up with Europe. . . . European achievements, European techniques, and the European style ought no longer to tempt us and throw us off our balance."[15] The rejection of imitation is absolutely crucial in a strategy of dissociation. This reliance on indigenous, creative resources for the generation of an alternative development model requires not only economic but also cultural dissociation.

CULTURAL DISSOCIATION

To move to the central theme of this chapter, the plea for cultural dissociation is based essentially on the thesis of Senghaas, as elaborated above. Applying this thesis to cultural development implies that cultural emancipation of satellite countries will be possible only through dissociation from the existing metropolis-dominated relations. Without cultural dissociation, all proposals for cultural emancipation are bound to remain new wine in old vessels. This is implicitly true as well for the new international information order. If the search for this order is not complemented with a plea for cultural dissociation, inevitably the choice is made for the integration model. This model might bring minor marginal improvements, but it will integrate Third World countries in an international system that operates against their very interests, impedes their emancipation, consolidates existing dependency relations, and both creates and legitimizes cultural synchronization.

In the current political debate, the new international information order is discussed mainly from the perspective of integration, which is the case for representatives of both industrialized and Third World countries. The integration model proposes that the satellite countries be enabled to participate more fully in an information exchange designed and controlled by the metropolis, to take place through the greater transfer of funds to establish, for example, national news agencies, technology for the technical infrastructure for such agencies, and expertise for the training of journalists.

In such a transfer, the organizational and professional standards of metropolitan information media are decisive. When Third World countries are lured into accepting such offers, which are often highly attractive, they are involved in a perpetual catching-up strategy. If one examines closely the process of transfer of advanced information technology, it is clear that this is an utterly senseless objective. The technological level of metropolitan countries is moving so fast that the satellite countries can only race after them breathlessly. Even if catching up were possible, one would still wonder what meaning this could have for an independent national development. For independent development, it is not decisive whether all countries participate in the international system with equal levels of volume and sophistication in technical advances; it is crucial, however, whether the scope, volume, and technical design of their contributions are determined by their own political, economic, and cultural priorities. Whether or not the exchange is exactly balanced is of secondary importance.

In this respect, the emphasis in the present international debate on the concept of balance is somewhat misleading. The new international information order stands for an information exchange in which all parties participate with inputs and outputs that are appropriate to their particular situations and not necessarily balanced in quantity or quality with the inputs and outputs of the others. The new international information order stands for a system of nonhierarchical relations between the participating nation-states, whereas a balanced system is not necessarily nonhierarchical.

One could imagine situations in which exporting information is very important for country A but less important for country B. In a certain phase of its development process, a country could feel the necessity to isolate itself from the international information exchange, precisely in view of its cultural emancipation.

The integration model is the very opposite of the dissociation model. The central argument of the latter is that an interindependent international system requires states to develop self-reliantly, which necessitates sovereign control of resources, including information. Only in this way can a state become independent not only *culturally* but also *economically* and *politically*.

For the development of an autonomous *cultural* system, it is essential that instrumental, symbolic, and social adaptive mechanisms be maintained and/or designed so that they are adequate vis-à-vis the specific environment. In order to achieve economic liberation, it is vital that Third World countries present their own version of their development problems and independently provide information about raw materials, import-export relations, technology, labor conditions, activities of transnational corporations, etc. Moreover, controlling the export of crucial economic information is necessary if a country wants to take national decisions without foreign influence. This has become very critical with advances in the international computer data traffic and satellite telecommunication channels.[16]

Sovereign control of production and distribution of information is also pertinent for *political* emancipation. Activating the total population to participate in the national development inevitably demands important contributions from the national information system.

Cultural dissociation, like economic dissociation, cannot be equated with total autarchy. The main goal is autonomous and self-reliant development; consequently, a task with high priority is that of liberating the country from the conditions that were designed to meet the needs of the metropolis. Dissociation is meant to create the necessary space to take inventory of national resources according to one's own concept of development and to exploit these independently. Dissociation is a prerequisite for the active social involvement of the people in national independence movements. Otherwise, to use the phrase of Gandhi, the people will be "blown off their feet" in the fragile beginnings of independence by the overwhelming presence of the powerful metropolis. As in the case of the feminist liberation movement, this implies that there is a decision to engage in struggle under rules that are not set by the opponent but are determined autonomously.

The concrete realization of dissociation may differ according to the various stages of development in which dependent parties find themselves. The different types of metropolis-satellite relations may also require quite different processes of dissociation. In all cases, however, it is of crucial importance to accept dissociation as the guiding principle.

This proposal for cultural dissociation may be summarized in terms of five major points:

1. It is a process in which a country chooses to disengage and delink itself from international relations that hinder its autonomous development.
2. It is an active choice *against* imitation of foreign cultural systems and *for* design of a cultural system adequate for a country's specific environment.
3. It is a series of strategies which will counterbalance the dimensions of cultural synchronization described in Chapter 1 and which imply precisely the opposite of the tendencies toward cultural synchronization.
4. A key requirement in the process of cultural dissociation is a national information policy which establishes a new pattern of international information relations. The national policies which imply interdependence in unequal relations and a type of technology transfer which is a perpetual catching up are rejected in favor of policies of interindependence. A country starts with the principle of self-reliance and selects elements that are conducive to long-range cultural autonomy. National information policy may be looked on as the cornerstone of cultural dissociation because information flows and information technologies influence so profoundly cultural development.
5. Finally, cultural dissociation demands four crucial components in a national information policy that halt the process of cultural synchronization: autonomous definition of a country's fundamental needs, formulation of policy principles based on these needs, translation of these principles into concrete planning, and mobilization of indigenous resources.

It is a fundamental premise of this study that the movement toward a new international information order can contribute to real Third World autonomy in global communications only in the degree that national information policies incorporate these principles of cultural dissociation. In the perspective of dissociation, a new international information order can be defined as an international exchange of information in which states that develop their cultural system in an autonomous way and with complete sovereign control of resources fully and effectively participate as independent members of the international community.

The first and decisive step toward a new international information order has to be the Third World countries' choice for their own independent information policy. National policies must also plan regional forms of cooperation so that the mutual support of a block of countries will provide a stronger base of information exchange and stop the divide-and-conquer strategy of the more industrialized countries.

NATIONAL INFORMATION POLICY

At the beginning of the 1980s, many Third World nations were beginning to be aware of the need to design and implement national information policies.[17] As the International Commission for the Study of Communication Problems (the MacBride Commission) has recommended in its report, "It is essential to develop comprehensive national communication policies linked to overall social, cultural and economic development objectives."[18] The commission has stressed as essential for policy making the democratic participation of all social groups concerned. Moreover, as the commission states, "every country should develop its communication patterns in accordance with its own conditions, needs and traditions, thus strengthening its integrity, independence and self-reliance."[19]

In the analysis of the present study, the concept of cultural dissociation fulfills most of the conditions as a guiding principle for the development of a self-reliant information system.

In general, this study prefers the phrase national *information* policy to that used by the MacBride Commission, national *communication* policy. Although no fundamental differences are implied, the concept of information is used for the following reasons. First, it corresponds better with the formula of a new international information order. Second, and more important, communication tends to be associated with mass communication only. In this study, the proposed policy making has to be comprehensive, encompassing also point-to-point forms of information transfer, as, for example, in informatics. Moreover, such policy making should address not only problems of infrastructure but also those relating to the information contents that these infrastructures carry.

In establishing a national information policy, the following elements appear to be essential:

- Definition of the *function* of the information system
- *Resource inventory*
- *Design of the structure* of a national information system
- *Control*, that is, the rules and mechanisms by which the internal and external functioning of the system can be controlled

These elements are all interrelated, as Figure 2 shows. This is a schematic model, to be interpreted as a prescriptive plan to be applied exactly in the form of the model. It is important, however, that all the

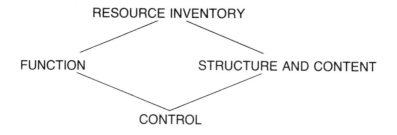

Figure 2   The Elements Necessary for Establishing a National Information Policy

elements be taken into consideration in any plan so that each factor reinforces the others. In the formulation of the information policy, objectives have to be clearly defined. Resources necessary for the achievement of these objectives have to be carefully analyzed. Resources and policy objectives have to be matched in light of overall developmental goals and principles. In the implementation of the information policy, resources will have to be deployed so as to create infrastructures and software that meet the defined objectives. For the evaluation of the information policy, some form of monitoring has to be established through which corrections and adjustments are made possible.

Function

Every society has to define, in one way or another, the crucial functions of information processes in that society as well as a description of the function of social institutions that carry these information processes. This is all the more urgent in Third World societies because of the severe problems that jeopardize the development processes both internally and externally.

As was noted above, information processes often critically hamper autonomous development by introducing inadequate forms of adaptation to the environment. Early in the planning process, it is important to examine carefully how information processes contribute to the shaping of techniques, symbols, and social patterns that enable a society to adapt to the needs of its particular environment.

For example, in many Third World countries, information processes, such as advertising, carry messages that induce people to acquire goods and services which bear no relation to real needs. Think of the many luxury articles pushed by advertising throughout the Third World. These goods and services often take on an added value beyond their intrinsic exchange value. They symbolize a status that people aspire to, and in almost magical fashion, they promise to fulfill dreams that many people could never realize through their own efforts.[20] As symbols, these goods and services satisfy real psychological and social needs. For example, a Mexican household may save a whole week in order to enable the father to drink Coca-Cola during the weekend. This is important because Coke has become a symbol that satisfies a genuine need for status and identity.

Such intangible needs are important in the lives of all persons and it is therefore perhaps preferable to look for products that can satisfy these needs and at the same time bring substantial benefits. For example, fruit juice might well be a more nutritious refreshment and also be given a symbolic meaning that is associated with status and identity. Such is the case if the native drink comes to symbolize the resistance to cultural annihilation and the search for Mexican identity.

The general function of the information process—achieving adequate adaptive relations—has three important dimensions: political participation, autonomy of minorities, and national integration.

Political Participation

The design of any national policy must begin by asking, "What kind of society do we want and how do we want to achieve this?" The answer will be decisive in defining the contribution to be expected from information processes.

Deciding on the most desirable societal structure must also take into consideration the existing political, economic, and cultural structures of the country. Usually some national political goals will have been formulated already and a specific type of economic system will be functioning. At times, a country may have a heavy overlay of imposed foreign culture, especially in Westernized urban enclaves; in most countries, however, more or less adequate cultural adaptive relations have evolved and have been sustained. In general, such political goals, economic systems, and cultural adaptive relations have been determined without a decentralized process of decision making which permits a wide base of popular participation.

Paolo Freire has observed that development cannot be realized in conditions of "silence."[21] This suggests that a plan for national development can be meaningful only if decisions about the distribution and execution of political power, the organization of production and distribution of goods and services, and the development of adequate techniques, symbols, and social patterns have been reached with extensive participation.

For any development process, it is vital to have horizontal information channels that activate all sectors of the population and that facilitate access to decision making for otherwise excluded sectors. The strategy regarding the national economic organization will have to be guided by what the people themselves indicate as their basic needs.[22]

In most Third World countries, the current economic organization certainly is not geared to these basic needs. An essential function of information processes is to make people conscious of this fact and to point to alternatives.

Cultural Autonomy for Minorities

As was noted in Chapter 2, some forms of liberation from dependence only install within a country another dominant elite who impose a condition of dependency on minorities. For this reason, it was stressed that national liberation movements are completed not simply with the removal of external dependency but simultaneously with a process of eliminating internal inequalities. As a country achieves self-reliance, there must also be the flexibility that allows different social groups to develop their specific adaptive relations.

Therefore, in the formulation of policy, a pertinent question is whether the efforts to achieve national cultural autonomy may jeopardize the cultural expression of regional or ethnic groups. Can national information policy sufficiently take into account the needs and aspirations of national minorities — the Fourth World within the Third World? This is a particularly difficult question, since national information policy will also have to take seriously the objectives of national integration.

National Integration

Encouraging the use of information processes for the expression of strongly contradictory interests may very well be a luxury that only highly developed and socially integrated nations can afford.

Many new nations have recently been formed that contained quite disparate ethnic and language groups, many of which have been geographically isolated from one another and for a long time have had separate cultural identities. The lack of a communication and transportation infrastructure, a condition typical of many underdeveloped countries, tends to reinforce such cultural isolation. Governments in these nations must seek a delicate balance between bringing these groups into a unity and at the same time respecting their minority cultures. Vital for such unity is the mobilization of all available resources and equitable distribution of them among all social groups. In a country which has a low level of developed resources to distribute in the first place and must carefully motivate a people to exert a coordinated effort, open encouragement of rancorous debate needlessly exacerbates divisions and courts disaster. At such a point the developing country finds itself in a situation significantly different from that of the advanced industrial state. The laborious and delicate process of development can afford only a minimum of internal contradictions to retain some potential for warding off the external pressures.

The more power that developing nations can exert in international relations, for example, through coordination with other nations in movements such as the nonaligned countries, the greater the flexibility in allowing internal minority autonomy. But when a nation has little power and is experiencing debilitating internal conflict, it is vulnerable to external intervention and consolidation of external dependencies.

Internal contradictions impede the development process and invite external intervention, which, in turn, reinforces the transnational cultural synchronization that hampers self-reliance and aggravates national disintegration.

National information policy has to promote national integration—not at the cost of monopoly by certain social classes but through balanced participation of all social sectors.

Taking Inventory of National Resources

Before translating the functions of a national information system into a concrete organization, technical infrastructure, and content, it is necessary to analyze both the availability and the form of adaptation of resources. When cultural autonomy is a major criterion, it is methodologically important to consider resources in terms of three categories: resources which are an integral part of the national context, resources already imported and adaptable to the national needs, and foreign resources which must still be imported.

National Resources

The way in which the critical functions described above can be implemented in specific national contexts depends very much on the nature and availability of existing resources—both physical and cultural—or resources that the country can at least produce within its limits.

If functions such as participation and autonomy are to be respected, it is important to consider whether elements from the indigenous national tradition can be exploited as contributions to an adequate adaptation to the environment. Traditional social values and institutions which underlie the cultural patterns of a country can often be most effective in the national development process, especially for gaining participation of large groups of the indigenous population. In the highland areas of Peru, for example, institutions rooted in the Inca past were revived to provide the organizational basis of a socialist society. In some countries there have been attempts to reintroduce traditional technologies which are better adapted and more economical in their specific situation. An example is the return to certain Indian medical practices in Mexico or the integration of folk doctors in the modern health care system of Zimbabwe. Another example is the study of the application of Inca irrigation systems on the upland plains of Peru.

For planning information processes, a key factor to take into account is that the basic resource, information, is already present within the national system and is controlled by the people themselves. This cultural resource is built out of the knowledge, experience, events, and historical developments present in every society. Every society also already possesses a great variety of traditional cultural symbols through which information can be expressed and exchanged in ways especially meaningful and comprehensible to the people of that country or region. This information exchange is supported by traditional techniques and communication channels which may be especially effective for the massive distribution of information precisely because they exist at the level of local communities throughout the country and because the people know how to use them without special training.

In many Third World countries these traditional forms are the living carriers of the cultural system that contributes in a relevant way to national consciousness. These are often more effective and more credible than are the modern information media because they are part of the native culture and use the language of the people. These traditional media often demand more active participation than do the modern mass media, facilitate interaction and feedback, and are more economical.

In some cases these forms can be very successfully combined with modern media. In Thailand, for example, the folk opera singers (maulum) maintain an important national tradition through their stories and songs on radio and television programs. In Senegal the "griot" (singer) keeps the national history alive through songs broadcast on radio and television.

Attempts to combine traditional and modern forms, however, raise the question of whether these expressions, which often have a sacred or literary context, can be tastefully and effectively used for contemporary social and political goals. In India, for example, villagers were enraged when the text of religious Yellama songs were adapted as a form of education or birth control.

A combination of old and new is feasible when the traditional form is flexible and open to improvisation. Examples are the Wajang Kulit performance in Indonesia, the clowns in the Nautanki play in India, the Indian story telling (Katha) and puppet theater (Kathputli), the puppet shows of Iran, the Egyptian ballads (cham soun), the comic stage play in Ghana (Kakaku), the folk music of Mexico (canción popular), and the calypso of the West Indies. These are all information processes that are readily available and embedded in a national cultural tradition. They must be considered important elements of an effective and authentic national information system.

Finally, in all Third World countries, the most important resource — human labor — abounds. In capital-short conditions, people can be engaged in achieving national information processes in place of expensive and often ill-adapted equipment.

Professional personnel should be local people who understand their indigenous audience well. Their training, insofar as is possible, should be planned and executed by local people in accordance with the level of expertise available in the country. For most of the information processes, Third World countries can train their own personnel with their own methods, professional norms, and social priorities.

It is often claimed that Third World countries would have too little program material and too few competent personnel to fill their media. This claim is deceptive, because it is based on the demands imposed by the arbitrary norms of more developed countries. A shortage of material and personnel is a problem only if one feels it is necessary to program more broadcast hours than the available material and personnel permit. Thailand provides a good example. When television was introduced in the late 1950s, Thai television broadcasting time was very limited. There were no problems in producing sufficient programs with talented local dancers, singers, performers, and puppet players. Only when commercial interests forced an extension of television broadcast time were material and personnel in short supply. In order to fill the approximately 70 hours of programming per week, it became necessary to import programs from the United States and West Germany.

As these cases show, an essential condition for autonomy is the tailoring of demands upon the information media to fit the available resources.

Adapting Resources of Foreign Origin

Most Third World countries have a colonial or foreign-dominated past, and much of the initial organization or technology for information processing was introduced during this period of heavy foreign influence. If a country wishes to adopt a policy of cultural autonomy, then it faces the question of adapting the policy to present national goals. A decisive criterion is whether the foreign elements are inherently linked with dependence or are open to often radical transformations.

For example, the question Mexican and Algerian television producers have posed is whether television drama, a form imported from the United States, can express the ideals of the country's national independence movements or will it be a negative influence on national loyalties? Or the question from Mozambiquans: How can the colonizers' language be used to support national liberation?

Techniques introduced under colonial rule can be exploited for national revolutionary goals. Radio in Algeria is an example. In the early 1950s Radio Alger was *the* symbol of French colonialism and an instrument for the synchronization of Algerian culture with the French model. For the Algerian, radio was "Frenchmen talking to Frenchmen." After 1956 this changed radically. Radio became *the* means of communication for the revolution. The *Voice of Algeria* quickly changed the Algerians' attitudes regarding radio and led in a short time to technical control of this medium. Radio was no longer part of the colonial oppression; it became a symbol of liberation.[23]

Another example of the adaptation of techniques imported during the colonial period and now available in Third World countries is the printing press. Many countries have access to small and medium size local printing shops that have come to play an important role in national information processes.

Some Third World countries have also embarked upon the production of their own broadcasting equipment. They have developed the expertise to adapt previously imported technology and have then exploited this with local people and materials. In Pakistan, for example, transmitters for medium-wave broadcasting and control systems for radio studios are manufactured by the Pakistan broadcasting corporation. The transmitters meet international quality standards and the cost is half that of formerly imported equipment.

Importing New Technology

For most of their more advanced communication technology, developing countries must go abroad. Vendors of this technology argue that new technology will enable developing countries to cut costs and accomplish in a few decades what it has taken Western developed countries generations to achieve in communication infrastructures. For countries in a hurry to develop, this argument is an attractive one. Seldom, however, do they question sufficiently whether this technology developed primarily for an urban industrial society is relevant or adaptable to the often vastly different conditions of their lands. In the decision on the import of foreign technology, a major criterion should be whether this technology can contribute to autonomous development.

From the perspective of autonomous development, importation of television and even radio has often been questionable. These are one-way traffic media which do not encourage an active participation of their audience and which are unable to take into account with some seriousness the local needs and problems.

In searching for an adequate technology, it may even be more meaningful to choose more advanced media in some circumstances. New mobile miniequipment can be far more adequate than that of current television and film techniques. The cases of Tanzania and of India described earlier are examples of this. In 1974 and 1975 attention in India was directed toward an experiment with educational programs by satellite (SITE). A project with a very cheap, small-scale technique located in Uttar Pradesh was hardly noticed. A system of portable video equipment was designed to improve the information exchange between villagers.[24] In contrast with radio and television, this was a medium the villagers could manage themselves and through which they could express their own local problems. They quickly became accustomed to the technical requirements of the equipment, decided themselves upon the program content, and used the programs to discuss their real problems. Interest in the commercial films that were initially shown on the monitor slowly disappeared and gave way to a keen appreciation for the locally produced programs.

In terms of professional television standards, their programs may have been of lower quality, but as channels for public information exchange they were highly relevant.

Scientific research methods could play an important role in the inventory of national resources. Research is presently primarily concerned with problems, concepts, methods, and techniques designed in the metropolis. Moreover, social research, including media research, has become a carrier of cultural synchronization.[25] Third World countries will have to gain independence in this field through their own initiative. They will have to ask their own questions and find relevant answers through their own methods of research.

THE STRUCTURE AND CONTENT
OF INFORMATION PROCESSES

Structure

The structure of a national information system will have to be designed in relation to the critical functions and the available resources described above. Consequently, structure must take into consideration four aspects:

- National control
- Decentralization
- Avoidance of control by professional elite
- A diachronic mode of information exchange

National Control

In current international relations, national control over a country's information system is an absolute prerequisite for national sovereignty. As a highly integrated system of global communications develops, a clear plan for keeping within the country control of information systems becomes more urgent. At stake is a vital resource for national development that must be exploited in accordance with a country's own goals. Sovereign control of the resource information means that a society maintains its autonomy in decisions regarding the processing, use, and export of information. To maintain this national autonomy, it is possible to employ many different forms of ownership and administration. A country must decide whether information systems should be fully nationalized or whether different media and different types of services require different kinds of control structures.

In Nigeria, for example, there are three different categories of proprietary control. In category I—involving radio, television, newspapers, advertising agencies, cinemas, and film distribution—full ownership by nationals is obligatory. In the case of category II, affecting the printing of books and the publishing of books and magazines, 60 percent of the ownership must be national. Category III requires 40 percent Nigerian ownership. This includes the industrial manufacture of parts for computers, radio, and television sets, and the production of motion pictures for theaters and television.[26]

Other aspects of national control to be considered are decisions regarding allocation of public funds for the development of facilities for information production, fiscal policy (for example, taxation of information flows) toward foreign companies, price policy for information services, PTT tariffs on television and telecommunication, and regulation of information imports and exports.

Given the expected functions of information systems mentioned above, national control implies both wide public participation and benefits for all social sectors, because the development of the total society is at stake.

In the past several years sufficient empirical evidence has been collected to support the observation that in Third World countries the free-market mechanisms for the production and distribution of information have not been able to satisfy the basic needs of these countries.

Systems of ownership, administration, regulation, etc., must respect this public and social purpose of information in order to fulfill the people's right to inform and to be informed and to avoid serving the needs of only the privileged classes of society. Information processes in Third World countries are an important form of public service, comparable to the educational facilities. Society can delegate this service to specific social institutions but it retains the right to regulate the execution of the service.

It should be clear that in this reasoning, national *control* does not mean that a governing elite has exclusive power over the operations of an information system. In any discussion of the forms of control over the means of production, it is important to make a distinction between allocative and operational control—that is, the difference between the *ownership* of the means of production (including the long-range allocation of resources) and the *execution* of the daily production operations. In the Netherlands, for example, there is an editorial statute which attempts to maintain a clear separation between the two forms of control, that is, between owners and directors and editors and journalists. One could conceive of a system in which the state would have allocative control of the information media, with various social groups having the operational control.

This position evidently begs quite a few questions. Information systems under national control are prone to abuse; evidence of this abounds in many Third World countries. It is not unusual to find a type of government-controlled development journalism that is virtually propaganda for the governing elite and its projects. Here the viewpoint of Third World spokespeople often creates confusion when they strongly emphasize the need to receive good press coverage in the North. It should be clear from this analysis that such coverage is certainly not a priority and possibly may even be threatening for national development.

In the international debate much attention is paid to such phenomena; some even see them as the core of the problem. In particular, those who limit the discussion to the problems of international newsgathering and distribution contend that most difficulties would be solved if in Third World countries no more journalists were censored, jailed, or expelled. Problems of censorship, detention, and expulsion have to be confronted and should not be minimized. It is important, however, to place this question in a more balanced perspective.

1. The problems of censorship, detention, and expulsion are not exclusive to Third World countries; they occur everywhere and are not *inherently* linked with certain types of ownership struc-

ture of the information media. Abuse of information processes under national control is not an *inevitability*. It is rather a consequence of the level of national development; the dominant political structure; the economic organization; the state of the population's political consciousness; and the degree of external political, economic, and cultural pressure.

2. One must also take into consideration that many problems accompanying present political institutions have their roots in the colonial or neocolonial dependency situation. This is not to sanction these abuses in any way. But it must be pointed out that critical analysis has to focus on structures that cause the problems with the freedom of information in Third World countries. Criticism of Third World governments is often also offered by defenders of Western liberties who were very silent at the time these very governments were installed by Western interests.

3. In cases of censorship, detention, or expulsion, the governments concerned are not automatically violating the freedom of the press. In many Third World countries, Western journalists either have collaborated with intelligence services, irresponsibly and carelessly reported, or exported data which indeed should have been protected. One example of inaccurate reporting relates to Cambodia. In early 1977, international media such as *Newsweek, Time,* and *The Washington Post* published pictures of executions and forced labor under the Red Khmer regime. Different sources (among them the U.S. State Department) identified these pictures as fakes that were stage-managed in Thailand. It has also become known that some media (e.g., *The Washington Post* and *Time*) knew this before they decided to publish. Such behavior can hardly promote the case for press freedom in Third World countries. In some cases the individual journalist has gotten into difficulties through personal and irresponsible behavior, for which any government can expel even diplomats.

However important the preceding discussion may be, it does not touch upon the core of the problem. That is located in the inability of national governing elite to develop adequate cultural systems. The decisive question is thus: Which social classes control decision making? This, then, leads to the second characteristic of the structure — decentralization.

Decentralization and Participation

To prevent monopolization of information systems by a small but articulate and educated elite, the structure of information systems requires a broader and more democratic form of control. Public and social control of information processes demands a fully decentralized form of decision making that allows the whole population to participate, at least in some way. The public media have an important role in political consciousness raising (conscientization), which fosters the active involvement of all sectors of society and a more critical judgment about national developments.

Avoiding Control by Media Professionals

In the evolution of the public media over the past century or more, the ordinary citizens have come to think of themselves simply as passive observers. The media are seen as the private domain of a small group of stars and professional producers.

One of the central proposals of the new information order challenges this form of the public media not only in the developing but also in the more developed countries. Structural decentralization in the information system means that the ordinary person sees his or her participation as a form of public service. It also signifies taking exclusive control of the information processes out of the hands of a professional elite.

The administration and operation of a national information system require recruiting and training individuals who have special talents for such jobs. However, once information is defined as the unique capacity of an elite group—separated from the rest of society even by its lifestyle—then the very structure of the information system gives a few specialists the exclusive right to inform nonspecialists.

Deprofessionalization means making an effort to guarantee everybody's right to inform and to be informed. It comes closest to the learning situation proposed by Paolo Freire. In his thinking, the conventional separation between instructor-specialist and pupil must be abolished. He assumes that everyone has knowledge and information about a part of reality and he advocates a situation in which everyone can give a contribution. In this perspective, the discovery of our reality can come about only through a creative process of co-learning.

Introducing a Diachronic Mode of Information Exchange

Every society is characterized by a complexity of information processes and by the exchange of an immense variety of messages through such processes. In a very real sense, the processes of information exchange constitute society and faithfully reflect its power relations.

Those with a higher socioeconomic status, education, etc., tend to have a more central position within information exchanges and are more likely to receive more information—especially more *strategically* important information. Their more central access to channels also gives them a better chance to decide which messages will be exchanged, because they decide on the agenda. More importantly, they determine which contributions in the exchange will be decisive. Many information processes are related to situations in which decisions have to be taken and choices have to be made from various possibilities. The positions of the participants in such situations will largely determine which alternatives are taken seriously.

Insofar as information processes are a reflection of existing power relations, they will in general follow a synchronic mode. In this mode, there is a great distance between sender and receiver; the receiver is supposed to synchronize with the input from the sender. The sender becomes the specialist who alone can select, process, and distribute the messages. Messages are "prescribed" to the passive receiver who is expected to register and store them in his "archives."[27]

In the synchronic mode, there is no dialog that can possibly make the receiver an active participant in the process or enable him to question the message and search for ways to relate the messages to everyday reality.

This synchronic mode is totally inadequate for a decentralized structure of information processes. The emancipation of individuals and social groups demands a diachronic mode for information processes. In such a mode, the distance between sender and receiver is reduced to the minimum. Messages from all participants in the process are pooled in order to come to grips with reality jointly.

The diachronic mode implies a series of characteristics in the pattern of information processes:

- The information is organized in such a way as to make visible the structural relations of reality.
- There exists a clear relation between the information and the contextual situation of the participants in the process of exchange.
- All participants have access to the facilities for input and correction.
- Information and social action are integrally linked.

Content

The general criteria which guide content decisions in a national information system are suggested, in the first place, by function, resources, and structural characteristics. Since the underlying criterion for these dimensions of information systems is national autonomy, this will ultimately influence the choice of content most significantly.

Self-reliant development presupposes liberation not only from external oppression but also from the *mentality of the colonized*. For the oppressed, paradoxically, to be human is to be an oppressor: the oppressor has become the model of humanity.[28]

At the same time, the oppressed looks at himself through the eyes of the oppressor and depreciates himself. "Self-depreciation is another characteristic of the oppressed, which derives from their internalization of the opinion the oppressors hold of them."[29]

In the process of liberation from these alienating images, information processes play an important role. Their content has to be oriented toward a liberation which leads to an authentic self-image.

If information processes are to contribute to liberated and self-confident acting, the implication for content is that:

- It facilitates the understanding of the environment in which people live ("What is your own life situation?").
- The mechanisms which determine and maintain the environment become transparent ("How is your own life situation structured?").
- Alternatives are offered for action leading to change ("How can your life situation be changed?").

As an example of how the content of information processes contributes to a more adequate understanding of the environment and greater freedom of choice, we can take the problem of hunger, which afflicts so many millions of poor in the Third World.[30]

Information on food problems in Third World countries could concentrate on the following:

1. Discovering with those concerned (especially the rural population) how their present situation is controlled by inaccurate *presuppositions* (such as the belief that hunger is caused simply by scarcity of food or by there being too many people)
2. Exploring how *real problems* are obscured through these inaccurate presuppositions (for example, the problem of exporting too much of food produced in the country, control of land resources by a small group that has no interest in feeding the whole population, or the import of modern agricultural techniques that benefit only a tiny elite)
3. Analyzing which *structural* causes underlie these problems (for example, the control of the national bureaucratic decision making by an elite that resists basic land reform, or the control of food production and distribution by a small number of large producers)
4. Designing *alternative* courses of action (for example, each country has the resources to minimize or solve the hunger problems

of its population, or the food production has to be directed primarily toward the population's own needs)

In the case of hunger, such information content is contributing to a more adequate adaptation to the environment and thus to cultural autonomy of the nation.

Control

The final dimension to be considered in planning a national information system is control of that system in accordance with national goals. Controlling the functioning of an information system is a universal characteristic of all societies regardless of the political-economic system or guiding philosophy. It will be found in free or totalitarian, developed or underdeveloped societies. It is simply an aspect of the general social controls that reflect the dominant cultural value orientations of a society. Every society has laws and rules to protect itself against the production and distribution of information that violates the moral and public order, state security, and national social institutions.

Again, the basic criterion of control is the national autonomy as well as respect for the culture of minorities and the right of the individual to be informed and to inform.

Such control mechanisms can be internal as well as external. Internal regulation determines whether the functions that are defined for the information system are indeed met. External regulation includes a variety of international agreements that have an impact on the national information system, such as telecommunication tariffs and frequency allocations. A combination of internal and external regulations is found in cases where rules for the national system are expected to have validity for the international system as well. In Mexico since the beginning of 1978, the international information flow is subject to all national laws regulating the domestic information flow.

Regulations and mechanisms for sanctions can be voluntarily imposed by those directly responsible for information processes, for example, through journalistic professional codes and press councils. Another possibility is for the state to legislate norms and check on their implementation. Finally, the audience itself can organize in consumer unions and take action.

In the international debate it is fashionable to criticize Third World countries for excessive controls that violate the right to know and to inform. It would only be fair to add that the industralized countries themselves have not found satisfactory solutions to this problem. The freedom of information only too frequently is used by professionals in the information field without sufficient responsibility. The influence of the state is often indirect and ambiguous. Critical consumer actions in the information field are weak or are easily thwarted by powerful political and/or economic interests.

For Third World countries, the key issue once again will be that of determining which rules and sanctions are adequate from the perspective of their own priorities and objectives. It is essential that the national information system meet its functions as defined. A society has to be able to judge and correct this. The opportunity to participate in this should be open to all social groups concerned.

Controls will also be applicable to the foreigners who participate in the national information system. They will at least be required to not disrupt the national development process.[31] Inherent in the right of a nation to its cultural autonomy is also the right to expect respect for the rules a nation designs to realize this autonomy.

A sovereign state will also want to design rules for the regulation of the international information traffic.[32] Codes of conduct will have to be developed to regulate the activities of both governments and private corporations.

In the next two decades more detailed and careful planning of national information systems may well become as central in the development strategies of most countries as is economic planning now. It has been the thesis of this chapter that an information policy guiding this planning must be built around a choice for cultural dissociation. Otherwise, the worldwide tendency toward cultural synchronization will increasingly threaten cultural autonomy.

The last part of this chapter will examine the main considerations for the application of the dissociation policy in the case of one of the most important new computer-like information developments—informatics.

INFORMATICS AS A CASE STUDY OF NATIONAL INFORMATION POLICY

The previous section outlined a general model for a national information policy. The broad guidelines were suggested in terms of four dimensions: function, resource inventory, content, and control. The basic criterion is achieving and maintaining cultural autonomy through a strategy of cultural dissociation. Underlying this strategy of cultural dissociation is the need for a parallel economic dissociation. This reflects the intimate relation that the international discussions have seen between the new international information order and the new international economic order.

All this has been presented at a relatively abstract level, however. The implementation of this model in concrete circumstances will vary a great deal in different societies and at different stages of social and economic development. A universally valid blueprint cannot be given.

It is possible, though, to point to the concrete questions that a Third World country confronts in formulating national information policy. Computer communication, or informatics, offers a good case study for a number of reasons:

- In present international relations, computer communication plays a significant role in cultural synchronization and poses a serious threat to national sovereignty.[33]
- Third World countries are at present confronted with highly attractive possibilities for becoming integrated in the international computer traffic. The Carter administration, for example, studied a plan to provide Third World countries with access to United States data banks. The costs involved for telecommunication channels and terminals would be covered by the United States.[34]
- The capacities of the advanced computer, especially through microelectronics, promise to make an impressive contribution to development processes.
- The applications of computers are manifold, which makes a selective policy possible. In India, for example, the computer is used as a "people supplement" where there is not sufficient labor. In sectors where labor is abundant, as in the case of banking, there is no electronic equipment (for example, no on-line banking).
- The computer can be very efficiently used in an extremely centralized system. At the same time, however, it can be adapted to specific personal and cultural characteristics (for example, learning speed or language) and thereby facilitate the participation of many people in decision-making procedures.
- The computer industry consists of various sectors, such as design and manufacture of equipment, maintenance and development, application of the uses of the equipment, and design of systems and programs. This also opens up the possibility of a selective policy.
- The case of the computer demonstrates that a self-reliant development does not necessarily imply exclusive interest for small-scale, indigenous techniques.
- The computer performs many functions at high speed, thus raising a question relevant to cultural values: How important is speed?

Taking computer communications (informatics) as a case study of national information policy is especially pertinent, because this is a new and vulnerable area of information flow. The dialectics between international economic and informational structures in the field of informatics deserve special attention.

Until recently, informatics and information have usually been dealt with as separate entities. Technological developments, however, make this separation obsolete. In a general way, information and informatics intersect at the point where informatics provides an increasing number of support services to information systems, such as computer-operated switching mechanisms to telephone systems or computer-operated sorting devices in newspaper mailing rooms. In a more specific way, the fields are related in a number of media applications of informatics, as Table 5 indicates.

The linking of information and informatics has many important implications:

- Information becomes strongly personalized ("atomization of information consumption"), i.e., due to increasing miniaturization.
- Information dissemination media become information retrieval systems.
- Computers become information/communication media.

The crucial element in the integrative process is the expected digitalizing of all types of information, which will make technical distinctions between data flows and information flows obsolete. Computer data and

TABLE 5   **Media Applications of Informatics**

Information	*Informatics*
Newspaper	Word processing and text composition
	Home terminal publishing
Magazine	On-line editing
Television	Computer-generated video
	Viewdata
Film	Graphics produced via computer
Radio and television	Computer-steered satellite transmissions
Educational publishing	Computer-assisted instruction packages
Telephone	Computer voice recognition
Telegraph	Data networks

journalistic information alike will be transmitted across borders in digital form.

The change from analog to digital form will have far-reaching consequences for the storage capacity and the transmission speed of information as well as for its accessibility and manipulation.

If present developments continue, the informatics-information link may well provide the vital stronghold for consolidating the power of the present international order. This may be particularly so in an application, sometimes described as "telematics," which links advanced telecommunications technology with electronic data processing. It has greatly facilitated the development of transborder computer-communication systems. These systems carry increasing volumes of information across national borders: medical, employment, criminal, and credit records of private citizens; credit data about commercial firms; and information about national economic developments. In fact, such transborder data flows have become the backbone of international business and banking.

Almost exclusively in control of this computer communications system are a small number of United States electronics corporations which have access to the technology that enables the collecting, processing, transmitting, and storing of enormous volumes of data. For many Third World countries this signifies that an important basis for national decision making is now located extraterritorially with some private corporation.

A spectacular element in this field is remote sensing by photo satellites. The "spy-in-the-sky" satellites can remotely sense the earth's surface in a country and by so doing "impede the exercise of the sovereignty of any state over its natural resources."[35]

Data extracted by these satellite explorations are processed by computer systems and stored in data banks, all controlled by the major Western transnational corporations. As Louis Joinet of France's Ministry of Justice stated in a speech to the Organisation of Economic Cooperation and Development (OECD):

Information is power and economic information is economic power. Information has an economic value, and the ability to store and process certain types of data may well give one country political and technological advantage over other countries. This, in turn, may lead to a loss of national sovereignty through supranational data flows.[36]

The dependent nations will find that even if they achieve significant progress in redressing inequality in international news exchange but do not gain self-reliance and sovereign control in the informatics field, equality and independence will remain empty diplomatic phrases.

The inclusion of informatics in programs of research and action related to a new international order is essential. The case of informatics provides an important illustration of both the necessity and the feasibility of a new international order.

The necessity is demonstrated by the fact that informatics in its present form constitutes a basic infrastructural component of the international economic and information order. The informatics industry is among the world's largest industries and is almost totally controlled by a few corporations located in the heart of the Western industrialized nations. Geared to the needs of these nations, it puts dependent, developing nations at a considerable economic and informational disadvantage.

Informatics opens up the feasibility of the new order in that it represents at the same time both the power and the vulnerability of the controlling nations. The business community of the industrialized world has become increasingly dependent upon telematics both for its information flows and its economic performance. Third World countries, apart from being potentially important informatics markets in the next decade, could seriously affect the economy of the industralized world if they restricted transborder data flows, imposed taxes on these flows, or indigenized informatics facilities.

These observations suggest a series of questions that a Third World country should ask when designing a national information policy:

- How does informatics contribute to the functioning of an information system? Will it further national disintegration? Will it introduce inadequate techniques, symbols, and social patterns? Will potential short-term benefits be outweighed by long-term deleterious effects?
- How will informatics relate to resources? Are they to be imported? Will this jeopardize national self-reliance? Can investments be brought in line with overall development priorities and needs? What does this mean in terms of the present allocation of human and financial resources?
- How will informatics be structured? Can a *national* production structure be organized? Will this contribute to self-reliant development? Will a strengthening of domestic informatics facilities lead to an improvement of international bargaining positions?
- How will informatics be controlled? Can the import and export of computer data be regulated? Can taxes be imposed on data flows?

These questions suggest that the design of a national policy for the informatics field should focus on the following elements:

- Since information technology is often introduced without specification of the objectives to be achieved by it, a priority would be the precise definition of a country's information needs.
- Technologies which are currently offered to Third World countries have to be carefully analyzed and matched against stated developmental objectives and information needs.
- Since information policymakers have often concentrated on the procurement of hardware only, careful analysis and projection ought to be made regarding the secondary impact of information technology, in terms of the distribution of political, economic, and cultural benefits.
- Careful attention has to be given to the institutional context within which the technology is applied. It will have to be studied whether present infrastructural arrangements are sufficiently solid to monitor and control the applications.
- Careful evaluation of the physical and human resources is needed to determine which resources can be developed independently, which can be mobilized collectively through regional cooperation, and which must be imported from developed countries with a minimum of external dependence.

As has been stressed throughout this chapter, delinking or dissociation, although central, is but one side of the coin in national information policy and planning. It must be complemented by building a new pattern of regional, horizontal linkages among developing countries. This need for regional cooperation is briefly analyzed in the next chapter.

REFERENCES

1. *Development Dialogue* (Uppsala), vol. 2, 1976, p. 9.
2. Jan Tinbergen et al., *Reshaping the International Order*, New York, Dutton, 1976, p. 111.
3. Jörg Becker (ed.), *Free Flow of Information*, Frankfurt, Gemeinschaftswerk der Evangelischen Publizistik, 1979, p. 215.
4. *Inter Press Service Newsletter,* January 1979.
5. Editorial comment in *Development Dialogue*, p. 10.
6. Tinbergen, *Reshaping*, p. 111.
7. Juan Somavia, "An End to Slanted News," *Development Forum (Geneva)* January-February 1978, p. 10.
8. R. D. Curtin, *The Image of Africa*, Madison, University of Wisconsin Press, 1963.
9. The Information Industry Association, representing the major information industries in the United States, defines information as a "resource" in its

report to President Carter 15 July 1977: "It [information] is the raw material of knowledge. . . it has a central role in the market place as a commodity." Information Industry Association, Bethesda, Md, 1977.

10. Documentation for these principles has been derived from: *Cocoyoc Declaration*, October 1975, Mexico; United Nations, General Assembly, 6th Special Session, May 1974, *Declaration and Action-Program on the Establishment of a New International Economic Order*, Resolutions 3201 and 3202; United Nations, General Assembly, December 1974, *Charter of Economic Rights and Duties of States, Resolution 3281; Dakar Declaration and Action Program of the Conference of Developing Countries on Raw Materials*, 1975. These documents can be found in G. F. Erb and V. Kallab (eds.), *Beyond Dependency*, New York, Praeger, Appendix B, pp. 185-250.

11. *Weltwirtschaftsordnung und Entwicklungspolitik*, Frankfort, Surhkamp, 1977.

12. Ibid., p. 215.

13. Ibid., p. 277.

14. Karl P. Sauvant and H. Hasenpflug (eds.), *The New International Economic Order*, Frankfurt, Campus Verlag, 1977, p. 5.

15. Frantz Fanon, *The Wretched of the Earth*, Baltimore, Penguin, 1967, p. 252.

16. See A. Gotlieb et al., "The Transborder Transfer of Information by Communications and Computer Systems," *The American Journal of International Law*, vol. 68, no. 1, 1974, pp. 227-257.

17. E. Lloyd Sommerlad, *National Communication Systems*, Paris, UNESCO, 1975; John A. R. Lee, *Towards Realistic Communication Policies*, Paris, UNESCO, 1976; Raquel Salinas, *Communication Policies: The Case of Latin America*, Stockholm, Institute of Latin American Studies, 1978.

18. Sean MacBride et al., *Many Voices, One World: Communication and Society Today and Tomorrow*, Paris, UNESCO, 1980, p. 254.

19. Ibid., p. 254.

20. "The fetishism of commodities lies in their prestige-value, in their ability as 'signs' to command respect, authority, deference." John P. Digging, "Reification and the Cultural Hegemony of Capitalism," *Social Research*, vol. 44, no. 2, 1977, p. 365.

21. Paolo Freire, *Cultural Action for Freedom*, Baltimore, Penguin, 1972, p. 17.

22. The concept of basic needs can be used as a paternalistic instrument in north-south negotiations in cases where the north defines for the south which these are. It can also be exclusively focused on national situations as a means of avoiding any structural changes in the international order. Basic needs in this study is used as a strategic concept for a developmental process in which needs are primarily and autonomously defined by the people concerned themselves; and the international order is structured in such a way as to make this possible.

23. Frantz Fanon, *A Dying Colonialism*, Baltimore, Penguin, 1970, p. 67.

24. Centre for Development of Instructional Technology (CENDIT) in New Delhi.

25. Cees J. Hamelink (ed.), *Communication Research in the Third World*, Geneva, Lutheran World Federation, 1976; Phillip Elliott and Peter Golding, "Mass Communication and Social Change: The Imagery of Development and the Development of Imagery," in E. de Kadt and G. Williams (eds.), *Sociology and Development*, London, Tavistock, 1974, pp. 229-254.
26. *Nigerian Enterprises Promotion Decree*, Lagos, Nigeria, Government Publishing, 13 January 1977.
27. Cees J. Hamelink, "An Alternative to News," *Journal of Communication*, vol. 26, no. 4, 1976, pp. 120-123.
28. Paolo Friere, *Cultural Action*, p. 22.
29. Ibid., p. 38.
30. Frances M. Lappe and J. Collins, *Food First*, Boston, Houghton Mifflin, 1977.
31. Recall the role of foreign media in Chile during the Allende government. NACLA, *Latin America Report*, vol. 8, no. 6, 1974; Herbert I. Schiller, *Communication and Cultural Domination*, New York, International Arts and Sciences Press, 1976.
32. Such rules have been accepted by the states that signed the Final Act of the Helsinki Conference on Security and Cooperation in Europe in 1975.
33. Burt Nanus, "The Social Implications of the Use of Computers Across National Boundaries," New Jersey, American Federation of Information Processing Societies, 1973.
34. "Global Net May Serve Third World," *Computerworld*, 26 June 1978.
35. UN Resolution 626, VII.
36. Given at the OECD Symposium on Transborder Data Flows and the Protection of Privacy, Vienna, October 1977.

5

Toward Regional and International Cooperation

A s was stated before, self-reliant development is not identical with
autarchy. Opportunities for cooperation with others remain, provided that they support the autonomy of the country.

It is essential that Third World countries realize such cooperation
primarily among themselves. National self-reliance is thus reinforced by
collective self-reliance.

The first collective performance by Third World countries dates back
to the 1950s. In that period many of them were engaged in the transition from a colonial to a postcolonial status. In those years the political
cooperation between African and Asian countries was particularly at
stake, as the 1955 Bandung conference demonstrated.

In the 1960s the coalition extended to include the Latin American
countries, which brought special economic problems to the agenda. Actually, since the mid-1960s, the nonaligned movement has given increasing attention to strategies for the development of economic links
among the countries of the Third World.

Alongside the nonaligned movement, the so-called Group of 77
came into existence at the First UNCTAD Conference in 1964. This
group, which in 1980 totaled some 122 countries, became the voice of
the Third World in United Nations forums.[1]

These two overlapping groups of countries indicate the ambivalent
position of the Third World: they find themselves caught between
strengthening horizontal linkages and coping with remaining links with

the metropolis. That these latter links also had an important cultural component became clear in the early 1970s. Particularly since the nonaligned summit in Algiers (1973), horizontal cooperation was also extended to the area of cultural emancipation.

The evident lack of success with these political, economic, and cultural forms of cooperation leads some participants in the discussions regarding international development to speak rather condescendingly about Third World collective performance. They are of the opinion that unanimity among Third World countries is impossible and that the whole concept of a Third World is useless. "You have to get rid of the concept, Third World. It has become very difficult to catch everything with one concept," states F. van Dam of the Dutch Ministry of Development Cooperation. In his analysis, the Third World has to be subdivided into groups of countries with varying stages of development; separate negotiations have to be conducted with each of these groups.[2]

It cannot be denied that efforts to achieve cooperation have not met with great success. The Third World is indeed not a homogenous entity. It is a rather heterogeneous collection of states with different priorities, social systems, and links to the key power centers of the world. Moreover, in many Third World countries, the national elites opt for integration in the international system and thereby frustrate the chances for independent national and regional development.

A meaningful and viable regional cooperation is possible only if the decision is taken to dissociate from the metropolis. Third World countries—complementing each other—could mobilize sufficient resources for a development, independent from the world market, not only for economic development but also for cultural dissociation.

There is no easy formula for regional or worldwide cooperation among Third World countries, but the following guidelines do provide some basis for policy:

- Participating states must execute an autonomous national policy.
- In regional cooperation, decision making has to be decentralized.
- Availability of resources at the regional level has to be analyzed with explorations regarding the intensive lateral exchange of information about training facilities, scientific research, technology, experiences in contracts with foreign firms, and successes and failures with traditional forms of information production and distribution.
- Available resources have to be exploited jointly, including sharing of facilities, exchange programs, mutual transfer of technology, and joint development of appropriate technology.[3]

- Finally, a strategy must be developed for the complementary exchange of resources among nations.

There are currently promising signs of increasing commitment from developing countries to engage in economic and technical cooperation among themselves. Such increased regional and interregional joint ventures can strengthen local capacity for self-reliant development and enhance conditions for collective bargaining power.

During the 1970s the share of Third World countries' trade among themselves in the total world trade increased from 3.5 percent in 1970 to 6.1 percent in 1979. Whereas between 1955 and 1970 the annual average growth rate of trade flows among Third World countries was 6.6 percent, which was well below rates of growth for other trade flows in the world, since 1971 the annual growth rate has been 28 percent.

There has been a particularly rapid increase in the trade of manufactured products. In 1978 the share of manufactured products in total trade among Third World countries was 52.7 percent, which compared with slightly over 25 percent in 1960 and 42 percent in 1970. Some manufactured products seem to have a strong potential for substituting for imports from the metropolitan countries. They include products for which Third World countries have an increasing industrial potential, such as consumer electronics (radio and television receivers), electronic components (transistors), and telecommunication equipment. There are, however, serious obstacles to overcome if this horizontal cooperation is to gain strength. Among the problems are the residual metropolis-satellite links that influence the direction of international trade, especially through preferential schemes offered by the metropolitan market economies and through various strings attached to aid programs. The deficiencies in transportation and communication infrastructures among the Third World countries are also impediments. The perennial problems of dealing with the balance of payments and of obtaining long-term credits add to the difficulties. Many Third World countries do not have adequate trade policies to foster cooperation among themselves, and exorbitantly high protectionist charges are imposed on products from other Third World countries.[4]

INTERNATIONAL EXCHANGE

> National consciousness, which is not
> nationalism, is the only thing that will give
> us an international dimension.
>
> **Frantz Fanon**[5]

International exchange has to be judged in the light of its contribution to cultural autonomy. The guiding principle in this is the cultural dissociation through which a country creates the opportunity to design and develop its own cultural system independently. This is the basis for an *inter-independent* system.

This independence can be strengthened regionally in order to achieve a collective, self-reliant development. Thus, the basis is laid for a decentralized interindependent system for the international exchange of information.

Such an international system ends Third World countries' dependence on what industrialized countries are willing to supply. Their development is no longer determined by the world market but by their own priorities.

Once again, this does not exclude the transfer of information, but information will always be selected according to its usefulness for the consumer. It is the responsibility of Third World countries to draw up their own shopping list and to know precisely what they can use from the international supply.

EPILOGUE ON COUNTERVAILING POWER

I am conscious of the possibility that the plea for cultural dissociation may meet the reproach of naivete. It is also clear to me that the alternative plea for integration will seem to many much more attractive and realistic. I am convinced, however, that the latter will undoubtedly maintain the "tutelage" of the Third World. *If* one is serious about cultural emancipation and cultural diversity, I see no other way except dissociation.

I am also conscious of the fact that current international relations of power will strongly discourage and frustrate this process. Therefore, cultural autonomy will come about only through fundamental changes in these relations, changes that basically oppose the immense interests invested in the existing international order.

The unwillingness to transform the existing order has been abundantly demonstrated over recent years. The UNCTAD V in 1979 in Manila illustrated the impossibility of reaching agreement on proposals presented by the Group of 77 on the reform of the international monetary system.

Again, at the Special United Nations Session in 1980, there was no agreement on the Group of 77 proposals for more equitable participation of the Third World in the international monetary decision-making organizations. At the 1981 annual meeting of the International Monetary Fund, the group representing the developing countries indicated the possibility of canceling IMF membership as a protest against sharpened conditions for countries receiving IMF loans.

I do not think that appealing to the common interests of metropolis and satellite in the creation of a new order will solve this conflict. A strategy that employs such motives as sound self-interest or mutual interest may mobilize a desire for marginal changes.[6] It will not change the structure of oppression in such a way as to enable the oppressed to become real human beings.

What is at stake in the present situation is the constituting of effective countervailing power against vested interests. That is a laborious process in which, in the words of Brecht, "the new comes about through the subversion, continuation and development of the old."[7]

In this process, every step counts, if the countries are moving in the right direction. This study is an effort to at least point to the right direction in the field of information exchange. If Third World countries can find a way to implement a new information order with the kind of orientation suggested here, this could be an important contribution toward a new international community of nations.

It will be a community in which people discover who they are, define what they need, and decide how to acquire this.

REFERENCES

1. For an analysis of the role of Third World countries in the United Nations during 1950 to 1968, see Frans Stokman, *Roll Calls and Sponsorship*, Leiden, Sythoff, 1977.

2. In an interview in the Dutch weekly *De Nieuwe Linie*, 1 February 1978; see also R. L. Rothstein, *The Weak in the World of the Strong*, New York, Columbia University Press, 1977.

3. For documentation on regional technological cooperation, see B. P. Menon, *Bridges across the South*, New York, Pergamon, 1980; B. M. Udgaonhar, "Science and International Cooperation," *Science Today*, January 1977, pp. 17-27; *Cooperation for Development of National Communication Resources*, UNESCO Document OPI-77XWS/4, Paris, UNESCO, 1977; Declaration on Technical Cooperation between Developing Countries, UNDP Meeting of Experts, Kuwait, 1977; I. El-Zaim, *Problems of Technology Transfer*, Occasional Paper 78/6, Vienna, Vienna Institute for Development, 1978; Y. Nayadamma, *Endogenous Development: Science and Technology*, Occasional Paper 78/3, Vienna, Vienna Institute for Development, 1978; A. Mattis, *Science and Technology for Self-Reliant Development*, IFDA Dossier 4, Nyon, Switzerland, IFDA, February 1979; F. R. Sagasti, *Financing the Development of Science and Technology in the Third World*, IFDA Dossier 8, Nyon, IFDA, June 1979; United Nations Conference on Science and Technology for Development, Vienna, 1979, *Science and Technology for Development*, Proposals from the Andean Group, Lima, Junta del Acuerdo Cartagena, 1979.

4. For a more detailed account of these trade statistics, see UNCTAD, *Trade among Developing Countries by Main SITC Groups and by Regions, TD/B/C.7/21, Geneva,* 20 September 1978; and TD/B/C/.7/45, Geneva, 21 May 1981.

5. Frantz Fanon, *The Wretched of the Earth,* Baltimore, Penguin, 1967, p. 199.

6. Willy Brandt et al., *North-South: A Programme for Survival,* Report of the Independent Commission on International Development Issues, London, Pan Books, 1980, pp. 17 and 20.

7. Bertolt Brecht, *Meti Boek der Wendingen,* Nijmegen, SUN, 1978.

Bibliography

Culture and Imperialism

Beltran, Luis Ramiro, "TV Etchings in the Minds of Latin Americans: Conservatism, Materialism and Conformism," *Gazette*, vol. 24, no. 1, 1978, pp. 61-65.

Burton, Julianne, and Jean Franco, "Culture and Imperialism," *Latin American Perspectives*, vol. 5, no. 1, 1978, pp. 2-12.

Carnoy, Martin, "Cultural Imperialism, Cultural Identity and Economic Development," paper prepared for UNESCO, Studies and Programming Division, Stanford University, October 1980 (mimeographed).

———, *Education as Cultural Imperialism*, New York, McKay, 1974.

Cruise O'Brien, Rita, *Domination and Dependence in Mass Communications*, Sussex, England, University of Sussex, 1974.

———, *Professionalism in Broadcasting*, Sussex, England, University of Sussex, 1976.

Curtin, Phillip D., *The Image of Africa*, Madison, University of Wisconsin Press, 1963.

de Cardona, Elizabeth, "American Television in Latin America," in George Gerbner (ed.), *Mass Media Policies in Changing Cultures*, New York, Wiley, 1977.

Fanon, Frantz, *A Dying Colonialism*, Baltimore, Penguin, 1970.

Flora, Cornelia Butler, and Jan L. Flora, "The Fotonovela as a Tool for Class and Cultural Domination," *Latin American Perspectives*, vol. 5, no. 1, 1978, pp. 134-150.

Freire, Paolo, *Cultural Action for Freedom,* Baltimore, Penguin, 1972.
———, Pädagogik der Solidarität, Wuppertal, West Germany, Hammer, 1974.
———, *Pedagogy of the Oppressed,* Baltimore, Penguin, 1972.
Golding, Peter, "Media Professionalism in the Third World," in J. Curran et al., *Mass Communication and Society,* London, Edward Arnold, 1977, pp. 291-308.
Janus, Noreen, and Rafael Roncagliola, "Advertising, Mass Media and Dependence," *Development Dialogue* (Uppsala), vol. 1, 1979, pp. 81-97.
Kumar, Krishna (ed.), *Transnational Enterprises: Their Impact on Third World Societies and Cultures,* Boulder, Colo., Westview, 1980.
Lee, Chin Chuan, *Media Imperialism Reconsidered,* London, Sage, 1980.
Mattelart, Armand, and A. Siegelaud (eds.), *Communication and Class Struggle,* New York, International General, 1978.
———, *La Cultura como Empresa Multinacional,* Mexico, Ediciones Era, 1974.
———, "Cultural Imperialism in the Multinational Age," *Instant Research on Peace and Violence,* Peace Research Institute of Tampere, Finland, vol. 4, 1976, pp. 160-174.
———, and Ariel Dorfman, *How to Read Donald Duck,* New York, International General, 1975.
———, *Mass Media-Ideologies et Mouvement Revolutionnaire,* Paris, Anthropos, 1974.
Memmi, A., *The Colonizer and the Colonized,* Boston, Beacon, 1965.
Reyes-Matta, Fernando, "The Information Bedazzlement of Latin America," *Development Dialogue,* vol. 2, 1976, pp. 29-42.
Salinas, Raquel, and Leena Paldan, "Culture in the Process of Dependent Development," in Kaarle Nordenstreng and Herbert I. Schiller (eds.), *National Sovereignty and International Communication*, Norwood, N.J., Ablex, 1979.
Sarti, J. "Communication and Cultural Dependency: A Misconception," in E. G. McAnany et al. (eds.), *Communication and Social Structure,* New York, Praeger, 1981, pp. 317-334.
Sauvant, Karl P., "The Potential of Multinational Enterprises as Vehicles for the Transmission of Business Culture," in Karl P. Sauvant and Farid G. Lavipour (eds.), *Controlling Multinational Enterprises,* Frankfurt, Campus Verlag, 1976, pp. 39-78.
Schiller, Herbert I., "Advertising and International Communication," *Instant Research on Peace and Violence,* vol. 4, 1976, pp. 175-182.
———, *Communication and Cultural Domination,* New York, International Arts and Sciences Press, 1976.
———, "Madison Avenue Imperialism," in R. L. Merrit (ed.), *Communication in International Politics,* Urbana, University of Illinois Press, 1972, pp. 318-338.
Wells, Alan, *Picture-tube Imperialism?*, New York, Maryknoll, 1972.

National Information Policy

Documents of the International Commission for the Study of Communi-
    cation Problems, Paris, UNESCO, 1979: 17, *A National Policy for*
    Balance and Freedom of Information; 23-27, *Surveys of National Legisla-*
    tion; 28, *Comparative Account of National Structure for Policy and*
    Decision-making in the Communication Field; 29, *Survey of Interna-*
    tional Structures for Policy and Decision-making in the Communication
    Field; 39 bis, *Relation between the Right to Communicate and Planning*
    of Communication; 42, *Mass Media and National Development;* 43,
    Towards a National Policy on Communication in Support of Develop-
    ment; 61, *Communication Planning;* 63, *A National Policy for Pur-*
    poseful Use of Information: Mass Media in the USSR; 64, *A National*
    Policy for Socialization and Self-management of Information.
East-West Communication Institute, *Planning Methods, Models and*
    Organizations for Communication Planning, 5 vols., Honolulu, East-
    West Center, 1977.
———— , *Papers of Seminar on Transnational Communication Enterprises and*
    National Communication Policies, Honolulu, East-West Center, 1978.
Final Report of the Intergovernmental Conference on Communication
    Policies in Latin America and the Caribbean, San Jose, Costa Rica, 12-21
    July 1976, COM/MD/38, Paris, UNESCO, 1976.
Final Report of the Intergovernmental Conference on Communication
    Policies in Asia and Oceania, Kuala Lumpur, 5-14 February 1979,
    CC/MD/42, Paris UNESCO, 1979.
Final Report of the Meeting of Experts on Communication Policies and
    Planning, 17-28 July 1972, Paris, UNESCO, 1972.
Final Report of the Meeting of Experts on Communication Policies and
    Planning in Asia, Manila, 4-8 October 1976, Paris, UNESCO, 1976.
Gerbner, George (ed.), *Mass Media Policies in Changing Cultures,* New York,
    Wiley, 1976.
Haight, Timothy R. (ed.), *Telecommunications Policy and the Citizen: Public*
    Interest Perspectives on the Communications Act Rewrite, New York,
    Praeger, 1979.
Hancock, Allan, *Communication Planning for Development: An Operational*
    Framework, Honolulu, East-West Center, 1978.
Intergovernmental Bureau for Informatics (IBI) and UNESCO, *Report on the*
    Intergovernmental Conference on Strategies and Policies for Informatics,
    Torremolinos, Spain, IBI, 1978.
Katz, Elihu, and George Wedell, *Broadcasting in the Third World,* Cam-
    bridge, Mass., Harvard University Press, 1977.
Lee, John A. R., *Towards Realistic Communication Policies,* UNESCO Reports
    and Papers on Mass Communication, no. 76, Paris, UNESCO, 1976.
MacBride, Sean, *Many Voices, One World: Communication and Society*
    Today and Tomorrow (especially Part IV, chap. 1; and Part V, I and II),

International Commission for the Study of Communication Problems, UNESCO. London, Kogan Page; New York, Unipub, UNESCO, 1980.

Middleton, John (ed.), *Approaches to Communication Planning,* Paris, UNESCO, 1980.

Nordenstreng, Kaarle, and Tapio Varis, "The Non-homogeneity of the National State and the International Flow of Communication," in George Gerbner et al. (eds.), *Communication Technology and Social Policy,* New York, Wiley, 1973, pp. 393-412.

Pavlic, Breda "NIIO and National Communication Policies," *Media Development,* vol. 27, no. 4, 1980, pp. 7-9.

Porat, Marc Uri, *Communication Policy in an Information Society,* paper presented at the Conference on Politics and Computing, London, March 1979.

Robinson, Glen O. (ed.), *Communications for Tomorrow: Policy Perspectives for the 1980s,* New York, Praeger, 1978.

Salinas, Raquel, *Communication Policies: The Case of Latin America,* Stockholm, Institute of Latin American Studies, 1978.

Schiller, Herbert I. *Communication and Cultural Domination* (especially chap. 4), New York, International Arts and Sciences, 1976.

——, "Authentic National Development versus the Free Flow of Information and the New Communication Technology," in George Gerbner et al. (eds.), *Communications Technology and Social Policy,* New York, Wiley, 1973, pp. 407-480.

Sommerlad, E. Lloyd, *National Communication Systems,* UNESCO Reports and Papers on Mass Communication, no. 74, Paris, UNESCO, 1975.

Tehranian, Majid, *Communications Policy for National Development: A Comparative Perspective,* Teheran, Iran Communications and Development Institute, 1977.

Willings, John A., "Planning Communication Policies," *UNESCO Chronicle,* vol. 21, no. 4, April 1975.

New International Information Order

Ayar, Farid, *Preliminary Ideas on the Foundations for the New International Information Order,* Beirut, Federation of Arab News Agencies, 1978.

Becker, Jörg (ed.), *Free Flow of Information: Information zur Neuen Internationalen Informationsordnung,* Frankfurt, Gemeinschaftswerk der Evangelischen Publizistik, 1979.

Bielenstein, Dieter (ed.), *Towards a New World Information Order: Consequences for Development Policy,* Bonn, Friedrich-Ebertstiftung, 1979.

Bourges, Hervé, *Décoloniser l'Information,* Paris, Editions Cana, 1979.

Documents of the International Commission for the Study of Communication Problems, Paris, International Commission for the Study of Communication Problems, UNESCO, 1979: Masmoudi, Mustapha, 31, *Call for a New International Information Order* 32, Osolnik, Bogdan, *Aims and Approaches to a New International Communication Order;* 33bis, El-Oteifi, Gamal, *Call for a New International Order;* 34, Hamelink, Cees

J., *The New International Economic Order and the New International Information Order;* 35, Pronk, Jan, *Some Remarks on the Relation Between the New International Information Order and the New International Economic Order;* 39ter, Martelanc, Tomo, *Right to Communicate and the New International Communication Order.*

Gonzalez Manet, Enrique, *Descolonizacion de la Informacion,* Prague, International Organization of Journalists, 1979.

Gunter, Jonathan F., *The New World Information Order,* Washington, D.C., Academy for Educational Development, 1978.

Hamelink, Cees J., *The New International Information Order: Obstacles and Opportunities,* Vienna, Vienna Institute for Development, Occasional Paper, 1980.

Hammarbert, Thomas, *New Information Order: Balance and Freedom,* Stockholm, Ministry of Education and Cultural Affairs, 1978.

Harris, Phil, "News Dependence: The Case for a New World Information Order," report to UNESCO, Paris, UNESCO, 1977.

——, *Putting the NIIO into Practice: The Role of Inter Press Service,* Rome, Inter Press Service Research and Information Office, 1979.

IDOC-International, "The New International Information Order," *Bulletin,* n.s., no. 4-5, April-May 1980.

Ignat, N., "The Decolonization of Information and Its Economic, Political and Cultural Implications," *The Democratic Journalist,* no. 3, 1978.

"Information and the New International Order," *Development Dialogue,* no. 2, 1976. Whole issue.

"International Information: A New Order?" Special symposium with Fernando Reyes-Matta, Mustapha Masmoudi, Rosemary Righter, Kaarle Nordenstreng et al., *Journal of Communication,* vol. 29, no. 2, 1979, pp. 134-198.

International Organization of Journalists, *Current Views on the World Information Order,* Prague, International Organization of Journalists, 1977.

Kroloff, George and Scott Cohen, *The New World Information Order,* United States Senate, Committee on Foreign Relations, 1977.

Mankekar, D. R., *One-Way News Flow: Neo-colonialism via News Media,* New Delhi, Clarion, 1978.

New World Order for Information, Tunis, Secretariat of State for Information, 1977.

Nordenstreng, Kaarle, "Struggle around 'New International Information Order,' " *Communicator,* October 1979, pp. 24-29.

Reyes-Matta, Fernando (ed.), *La Informacion en el Nuevo Orden Internacional,* Mexico City, ILET, 1977.

Schiller, Herbert I., "Decolonization of Information," *Latin American Perspectives,* vol. 5, no. 1, 1978, pp. 35-48.

——, *Whose New International Economic and Information Order?* Paper presented at the International Conference on Alternative Development Strategies and the Future of Asia, New Delhi, India, October 1979.

Sussman, Leonard R., "Third World/West Open Media Dialogue as UNESCO 'Radicalization' Proceeds," *Freedom at Issue,* vol. 44, 1978, pp. 20-28.

"Towards a New International Information Order," *Media Development,* vol. 27, no. 4, 1980. Whole issue.

Varis, Tapio, Raquel Salinas, and R. Jokelin, *International News and the New Information Order,* Tampere, Finland, University of Tampere, 1977.

Transfer of Technology

Cruise O'Brien, Rita, "Technological Factors in International Communication," *Media Asia,* vol. 5, no. 2, 1978, pp. 103-106.

Ernst, Dieter, "A Code of Conduct for the Transfer of Technology: Establishing New Rules or Codifying the Status Quo?" in Karl P. Sauvant and H. Hasenpflug (eds.), *The New International Economic Order,* Frankfurt, Campus, 1977, pp. 297-314.

—— (ed.), *The New International Division of Labour, Technology and Underdevelopment,* Frankfurt, Campus, 1979.

Guzzardi, Walter, "The Great World Telephone War," *Fortune,* August 1977, pp. 142-147, 150, 154.

Hamelink, Cees J., "Imperialism of Satellite Technology," *WACC Journal,* vol. 26, no. 1, 1979, pp. 13-17.

Intergovernmental Bureau for Informatics, *Considerations on the Transfer of Informatics Technology,* SPIN Document 208, Rome, IBI, July 1978.

International Institute for Environment and Development, *Mobilising Technology for World Development,* Report of the Jamaica Symposium, March 1979.

King, Alexander, "Use and Abuse of Science and Technology for Development," in A. J. Dolman and J. van Ettinger (eds.), *Partners in Tomorrow, Strategies for a New International Order,* New York, Dutton, 1978, pp. 182-192.

——, and Aklilli Lemma, "Scientific Research and Technological Development," in A. J. Dolman (ed.), *Reshaping the International Order,* New York, Dutton, 1976, pp. 260-273.

Mattis, Ann, "Science and Technology for Self-Reliant Development," IFDA Dossier, Nyon, Switzerland, IFDA, 19 February 1979.

Mowlana, Hamid, "Political and Social Implications of Communications Satellite Applications in Developing Countries," in J. N. Pelton and M. S. Snow (eds.), *Economic and Policy Problems in Satellite Communications,* New York, Praeger, 1977, pp. 124-142.

Nayudamma, Y., *Endogenous Development: Science and Technology,* Occasional Paper 78/3, Vienna, Vienna Institute for Development, 1978.

Pavlic, Breda, "Communication Policies and Transfer of Technology: A Neglected Issue," paper presented at the NGO Conference on Science and Technology for Development, Vienna, 19-29 August 1979.

Sagasti, Francisco R., "Science and Technology Policies for Development," IFDA Dossier, Nyon, Switzerland, IFDA, February 1979.

Schiller, Herbert I., *Communication and Cultural Domination,* New York, International Arts and Sciences, 1976.

Schumacher, E. F., *Small Is Beautiful*, London, Blond & Briggs, 1973.
UNCTAD, *Report of the Group of Governmental Experts on the Industrial Property System on the Transfer of Technology*, Geneva, 26 June 1978.
Zaim, Issam El, *Problems of Technology Transfer*, Occasional Paper 78/6, Vienna, Vienna Institute for Development, 1978.

Transnational Information Industry

Boyd-Barret, Oliver, "Media Imperialism," in J. Curran et al. (eds.), *Communication and Society*, London, Edward Arnold, 1977, pp. 116-135.
Golding, Peter, "The International Media and the Political Economy of Publishing," *Library Trends*, vol. 26, no. 4, 1978, pp. 453-467.
Guback, Thomas H., *The International Film Industry*, Bloomington, Indiana University Press, 1969.
Hamelink, Cees J., *The Corporate Village*, Rome, IDOC, 1977.
——, *De Mythe van de Vrije Informatie*, Baarn, The Netherlands, Anthos, 1978.
Mattelart, Armand, *Multinationales et Systemes de Communication*, Paris, Anthropos, 1976.
Monaco, James, *Media Culture*, New York, Dell, 1978.
Read, William H., *America's Mass Media Merchants*, Baltimore, Johns Hopkins University Press, 1976.
Schiller, Herbert I., *Mass Communications and American Empire*, Boston, Beacon, 1971.
——, *The Mind Managers*, Boston, Beacon, 1973.
Tunstall, Jeremy, *The Media Are American*, New York, Columbia University Press, 1977.
Varis, Tapio, *The Impact of Transnational Corporations on Communication*, UNESCO Working Paper SHC/76, Paris, UNESCO, 1976.
——, *International Inventory of TV Programme Structure and the Flow of TV Programmes between Nations*, Tampere, Finland, University of Tampere, 1973.

List of Abbreviations

AFP	Agence France Press
ANN	Asia-Pacific News Network
AP	Associated Press
CANA	Caribbean News Agency
CENDIT	Centre for Development of Instructional Technology (New Delhi, India)
CIESPAL	Centro Internacional de Estudios Superiores de Comunicacion para America Latina
FCC	Federal Communications Commission
FELAP	Federacion Latinoamericana de Periodistas (Latin American Federation of Journalists)
FTZ	Free Trading Zone
GATT	General Agreement on Trade and Tariffs
GTE	General Telephone & Electronics
IAPA	Inter-American Press Association
IBEC	International Basic Economy Corporation
IBI	Intergovernmental Bureau for Informatics
IBM	International Business Machines
ICAIC	Instituto Cubano Arte y Industria Cinematografia (Cuban Institute of Art and Cinematographic Industry)
ICDA	International Coalition for Development Action
IDOC	International Documentation and Communication Centre

IFDA	International Foundation for Development Alternatives
ILET	Instituto Latinoamericano de Estudios Transnacionales (Latin American Institute for Transnational Studies)
IMF	International Monetary Fund
INTELSAT	International Telecommunication Satellite consortium
IOJ	International Organization of Journalists
IPDC	International Programme for the Development of Communication
IPI	International Press Institute
IPRA	International Peace Research Association
IPS	Inter Press Service
ISIS	Resource and Documentation Service for the Women's Liberation Movement
ITT	International Telephone & Telegraph
JUNIC	Joint United Nations Information Committee
MCA	Music Corporation of America
NACLA	North American Congress on Latin America
NCR	National Cash Register
NGO	Non-Governmental Organization
NIEO	New International Economic Order
NIIO	New International Information Order
NWICO	New World Information and Communication Order
OANA	Organisation of Asian News Agencies
OECD	Organisation for Economic Cooperation and Development
PAFNA	Pan African News Agency
PTT	Post Telegraph and Telephone (the national authority for)
SITC	Standard International Trade Classification
SITE	Satellite Instructional Television Experiment
SPIN	Strategies and Policies for Informatics
UCIP	Union Catholique Internationale de la Presse (International Catholic Union of the Press)
UNCTAD	United Nations Conference on Trade and Development
UNDP	United Nations Development Programme
UNESCO	United Nations Educational, Scientific and Cultural Organisation
UPEC	Union de Periodistas y Escritores Cubanos (Union of Cuban journalists and writers)
UPI	United Press International
VID	Vienna Institute for Development

Index

141

CEES J. HAMELINK is a senior lecturer on international communication at the Institute for Social Studies, The Hague, Netherlands. He received his doctorate from the University of Amsterdam and has taught and lectured on international communication in Mexico, the USSR, the USA, Switzerland, India, Hong Kong, Belgium, and France. Hamelink has written numerous articles and books in both Dutch and English.